Art in Action

Art in Action

Guy Hubbard

Indiana University

Teacher's Manual
Second Course

HOLT, RINEHART AND WINSTON

AUSTIN NEW YORK SAN DIEGO CHICAGO TORONTO MONTREAL

Printed in the United States of America   ISBN 0-15-770043-7(8)

2 3 4 5 6 7 8 9 0−92 91 90 89

Table of Contents

Introduction

The content of *Art in Action* is built directly on a foundation of art instruction developed by Guy Hubbard. Dr. Hubbard strives to create books for self-contained art classrooms in which teachers may or may not have sufficient preparation in the teaching of art. *Art in Action* represents his latest refinement of this theory. The result is a book that can be successfully used by mature students in upper elementary grades, by average middle and junior high school students, and by high school students with little art background. *Art in Action*, then, can work equally well in a variety of classroom situations. The purpose of the teacher's edition is to present options that will meet these diverse needs.

Art in Action was originally published under the title of *Art: Discovering and Creating*. The goal of this first edition was the full individualization of art instruction. This goal has been retained in *Art in Action*. However, as stated in the previous paragraph, the goal has been expanded to include as many school situations as possible. Thus, those situations in which students are likely to benefit from more guided instruction are also addressed.

The Structure of the Book

The art content is organized into units of lessons based on the familiar art forms of design, drawing, painting, and sculpture. Since printmaking and collage share many qualities, they have been united into a single unit and so have ceramics, crafts, and textiles. The sixth and final unit consists of lessons selected from various areas of art and directs students to solve artistic problems that are primarily creative and expressive. The lessons in each unit generally progress from simpler, more foundational tasks to those that are more complex and expressive. In this way, students can progress through a unit from beginning to end.

The duration of middle, junior, and senior high school art courses varies considerably, however, and only rarely will students have enough time to complete even a single unit from the book. Moreover, art teachers are well aware of the need for adolescents to experience as wide a range of areas within art as time permits. Students in introductory art classes who discover new aptitudes for art or who have their existing interests reinforced are more likely to continue with their art education throughout their elec-

tive programs. To help teachers and students make suitable selections within the units, therefore, the lessons are grouped into *unit strands*.

Unit Strands

Each unit consists of two or three strands. The appropriate strand diagram (that is, the diagram representing the unit strand that includes the lesson being completed) is shown in each lesson of the student text. Students will always complete the strands for each unit in consecutive alphabetical order. (That is, upon completion of strand A, a student is instructed to proceed to strand B; upon completion of strand B, a student is instructed to proceed to strand C; and so forth.) Students do, however, have choices about which lessons within a strand to complete. If necessary or desirable, the teacher may make these choices instead. Decisions about the degrees of freedom students should have are best made by each art teacher, since what an individual or a group of students is likely to be able to undertake successfully varies from class to class. Other factors such as time, classroom space, and the availability of art materials will also play a part in this decision.

Using strands is easy once they are clearly introduced. The following step-by-step instructions and diagram for strand L (Unit VI) should provide such an introduction.

Strand L: Messages and Imagination

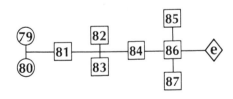

Step 1: Students will begin this strand by choosing and completing either lesson 79 or lesson 80.

Step 2: Students will complete lesson 81.

Step 3: Students will choose and complete either lesson 82 or lesson 83.

Step 4: Students will complete lesson 84.

Step 5: Students will choose and complete lesson 85, lesson 86, or lesson 87.

Step 6: The diamond-shaped symbol means that students should evaluate their own artwork and proceed to the next strand (in this case, strand M). Note: This symbol appears only in the strand diagram that is given for the last lesson in the strand—in this case, lesson 85, lesson 86, and lesson 87 would show strand diagrams with this symbol. At this point, students should review the lessons they have completed thus far, noting areas of improvement. They can also evaluate their own work by using the Learning Outcomes at the back of the Student Edition.

The Lessons

In order to make the lessons easier to use, a single format is employed. In this way both students and teachers quickly become comfortable using the lessons. Each lesson is clearly written at a level that students should be able to read without difficulty. In a very real sense, each lesson is not only an art lesson, but an exercise in reading comprehension as well.

Each lesson begins with a number followed by a title that provides an indication of content. This is followed by an introductory statement entitled "Observing and Thinking Creatively" that presents information about the art to be studied in that lesson. Next is a set of brief statements entitled "Instructions for Creating Art" which enumerate what the students are to do.

The reproductions to be found within each lesson are included because the foundation of all art studies lies with appropriate visual images. Some of the artworks reproduced within the lessons are by the recognized great artists of the world. Others have been selected from the great civilizations of the past, while still others are works by contemporary artists. Not least, quite a few images are examples of art by adolescents whose work illustrates the intent of a lesson. By means of such a wealth of examples, students are guided through one or more interpretations of a lesson to a clearer understanding of what is expected of them. These pictures have the indispensable function of introducing students to the visual literature of art. Many lessons use visual images to instruct students in art history and the content of criticism, often calling for the students to express their aesthetic feelings about the given art. In addition, all the images in the book contribute informally to the general education of the students by making them familiar with art in various media and with works from different times and places. These images collectively are, in short, a valuable resource for art education.

Goals that are explicitly instructional are served by diagrams of various artistic techniques, pictures of art in progress, and photographs of objects and places. Colored photographs also appear in many lessons to encourage students to observe and interpret both the natural and manmade environment around them.

Each lesson concludes with a list of needed art tools and materials. All these items are of a kind that are found universally in school art rooms, so that no student need be prevented from doing a lesson for want of the proper materials.

Learning Outcomes

Underlying the structure of the units, strands, and lessons is the subject matter of art. The content of the book has been selected from across the range of artistic subject matter. The objectives, or *Learning Outcomes* as they are referred to in the Student Edition, are the heart of the book. The main purpose of the school art program is for students to become educated in the subject of visual art. This means learning information about art as well as demonstrating the understanding that can only come about from the act of handling tools and materials to create art. An education in art also includes coming to value art. Thus, each lesson is based on several learning outcomes selected from these three areas of artistic content.

Anything verbal or visual that a student learns and remembers belongs in the category of *Understanding Art*. This includes words and their definitions, information about artistic techniques, historical information, and also images that a student sees and is expected to remember. The second category is *Creating Art*, and it includes all the learning that occurs when a student is actually producing art. This refers to all the skills a student is to learn, including various safety precautions that must not only be known (Understanding Art) but actually practiced. This category of learning includes most of what is found in traditional art lessons where art production is the primary focus.

Affective valuing is also a necessary part of any art program that claims to be comprehensive. In this book, these learning outcomes fall under the title of *Appreciating Art*. The focus of learning in this area lies with nurturing students' aesthetic values. Performance in this area usually means a visible development of the student's feelings about art through a recognizable increase in the abilities to make choices, orally express preferences, and coherently discuss the qualities he/she considers important in a work of art. It also means being held responsible for giving reasons for a particular point of view. Appreciation objectives in no way mean that student statements need correspond with what a teacher believes or with what is generally held to be the proper assessment of a work. To the contrary, the real task here is to develop a student's ability to reach personal conclusions and justify them. A word of caution is needed with appreciation objectives, however. Most adolescents are developing the abstract thinking skills needed for achieving these objectives, but many of them will not yet have advanced far enough to make complex aesthetic judgments. Moreover, the typical student's experiences with consciously engaging in this kind of thinking is modest compared with other kinds of abstract thinking behavior that receive much more emphasis in the school curriculum. Thus, it is important for you to understand a student's initial reticence during discussions and to work to build a rapport with each student which will enable him or her to confidently express opinions.

Since the study of art consists of content from all three areas of learning, whatever is learned in one area can be expected to affect learning in the other two. For this reason, an improved art vocabulary, together with visual recall of several important art-works is likely to influence a student's aesthetic response to a recently completed artwork by another student in the class. Similarly, the production experience of modeling with clay over an armature is likely to make a student more sensitive to the work involved in the production of a piece of professional sculpture that was executed in the same way.

In sum, the single most important concept in this book is that it is built on a foundation derived from the content of art that, with the help of an art teacher, most adolescent students are likely to be able to learn. Insofar as the content and the structure facilitate student needs, the book will prove to be useful as written. In some circumstances, changes will be needed—as with remediation. On those occasions, an art teacher will be able to do this more easily by modifying the content than by having to start from the beginning.

Evaluation

Evaluation in art presents difficulties that separate it from evaluation in other subjects. On the other hand, much of the art that can be learned may be evaluated in much the same way as in other subjects. The first step to managing the evaluation task is to be found in the statements listed at the end of the Student Edition under *Learning Outcomes*. Each of these statements either establishes what a student should have learned or calls for the student to respond in such a way that he or she shows what has been learned. If student performance is compared with these learning outcome statements, then evaluation is practical. For example, when students are asked to paint with various thicknesses of transparent watercolor, the finished painting will provide the needed information.

Similar comparisons can be made for knowledge about art and also for appreciating art. The methods used for determining achievement in these two areas are likely to include such things as having students, either orally or in writing, use particular words correctly in context or recognize the period of a painting. Also, they might either describe or draw an object that was to have been remembered. Learning in the area of appreciation usually calls for some kind of oral or written explanation that throws light on why students made a particular decision.

Art vocabulary is relatively easy to evaluate. It is apparent when a student defines a word accurately, spells it correctly, and uses it properly in context. Similarly, learning outcomes relative to historical knowledge as well as to skill with artistic techniques are relatively simple to evaluate. Students either know it or can do it to a level that is reasonable for adolescents—or they cannot. Degrees of knowledge and skillfulness are more difficult to assess, but setting standards for minimal performance normally does not present great difficulty.

Evaluation problems escalate dramatically when the task goes beyond skills and facts. If a student satisfies the stated criteria, then he or she has succeeded with that part of the lesson—but only at a minimal level. Evaluative decisions beyond this minimal level can only be made by teachers in the classroom. Only they have the knowledge and understanding to make more complete judgments about student work. For example, one student who has barely met the criteria for a given lesson may deserve special credit if he or she has a handicap that makes such an achievement difficult. In contrast, another student might far exceed the minimal objective and yet be credited with only marginal success because he or she has natural talent but did not apply it during the lesson. The objectives referred to in the learning outcomes, therefore, are intended only to point toward a desired direction. Only the art teacher is competent from that time on to judge the quality of a given performance by an individual student or an entire class.

Several other references to evaluation need to be made. The first has to do with learning outcomes that a teacher believes need attention but which are not mentioned in the book. Although lists of learning outcomes for each lesson are appropriate for the lesson as written, a teacher may see the need for some other objective to be achieved from that activity. In this case, it should be added or substituted in the Student Edition so students know what they are expected to learn.

Another departure from the book will occur when students show that they have learned something of value that was not asked for. For example, a student may use words in a particularly expressive way, or render gradations of curved forms in an especially sensitive way. It would be unfair to a student for such unexpected performance to be disregarded just because that particular outcome was not identified in the lesson. Evaluation at its best should give credit for what is learned, regardless of whether it was specified or whether it happens unexpectedly.

The need for evaluation also provides unique opportunities for enhancing student learning. During the original field testing of the program, and on several occasions since, students have taken turns using the learning outcomes to evaluate the work of their classmates. As long as the statements of what was to be learned are clearly stated, students make excellent evaluations. Moreover, the act of evaluating seems to compel student evaluators to master the content of the lesson more than they would when evaluated by their teachers. The student whose work was being evaluated, moreover, also tended to check more carefully that he or she had done everything that was expected before submitting the work for evaluation. The only problem with this strategy lies in the tendency for some student evaluations to be unnecessarily harsh; thus, the teacher must become a tempering influence. The benefits of peer evaluation are significant, however.

The *Learning Outcomes* are also useful tools for students to use to evaluate themselves. The individualized nature of the program naturally calls for some measure of self-evaluation. By referring to the learning outcomes upon completion of every lesson, students can actually check their own progress and recognize the areas that require additional work. The learning outcomes, then, are

inherently useful for the three types of evaluation: teacher, peer, and self.

Finally, a troublesome problem that the statements of learning outcomes help overcome is the tendency for some teachers to evaluate student work from their personal points of view without regard for the objectives of a lesson. When that happens, students rapidly learn that the only real criterion for success is to please the teacher.

Use of Critical Thinking Skills

The format of each lesson in *Art in Action* has been developed to elicit the use of critical thinking skills combined with creative observation. The title at the beginning of each lesson, *Observing and Thinking Creatively*, implies the significance of these skills in the process of art learning. The text for the lessons has been written inductively in order to relate to students' experiences, involve their active participation, and encourage higher levels of thinking.

Students are often asked to respond to the visual images in the lesson. These images fall into four different categories: artwork by master artists, representative students' artwork, photographs, or illustrations of methods and techniques. Captions are included for famous works of art that provide specific information about the artists, art styles, media, and techniques. The captions also encourage students to study the visuals to observe particular art elements and principles that make them noteworthy.

Following the visuals, specific step-by-step instructions guide students through the process of art production. These instructions are written so that most students can work independently, allowing the teacher time to meet with individual students or attend to other tasks. Further individualization is possible if students follow the art strand at the end of each lesson, enabling them to move ahead at their own pace. Before proceeding to the next lesson, students are encouraged to evaluate their work using the *Learning Outcomes* at the back of the Student Edition. (See the preceding discussion of *Learning Outcomes* for a complete description). As previously stated, the *Learning Outcomes* can function as a means for self-, peer, and teacher evaluation. An *Art Evaluation Record Sheet* on page XII has been included for this purpose. The *Learning Outcomes* have been written to encourage the use of higher level thinking skills and are based on Benjamin Bloom's *Taxonomy of Educational Objectives*.

Learning Outcomes
Correlated to Critical Thinking Skills

The Learning Outcomes for each lesson are grouped in a special section at the back of each student book. They are explained in detail on pages VI and VII of the Teacher's Manual. Students and teachers may refer to the Learning Outcomes after each lesson and use them as the criteria for evaluating art learning. The questions and statements included in the *Learning Outcomes* are based on the use of critical thinking skills as explained by Benjamin Bloom and his cowriters in *A Taxonomy of Educational Objectives in the Cognitive Domain*. The charts on the next few pages show the relationship between the *Learning Outcomes* and the six levels of thinking—knowledge, comprehension, application, analysis, synthesis, and evaluation.

KNOWLEDGE
Recall information learned in similar form
Behavioral Terms Indicating Knowledge:

list	repeat
define	quote
state	spell
name	recite
select	label
locate	identify
observe	memorize
show	match

Sample Learning Outcomes (Student Edition):

Leonardo da Vinci was a scientist and engineer as well as an artist. Name three things he invented or designed.
(Lesson 10; page 232)

Name three drawing instruments that can be used to make geometric art.
(Lesson 15; page 233)

Define the term perspective.
(Lesson 16; page 233)

Learning Outcomes Requiring Use of Knowledge:*

1.1, 2.1, 3.1, 4.1, 5.1, 6.1, 7.1, 8.1, 8.2, 10.2, 11.1, 12.1, 13.1, 14.1, 15.1, 15.2, 16.1, 17.1, 18.1, 19.1, 20.2, 21.1, 21.2, 22.2, 23.1, 24.1, 25.1, 26.1, 27.1, 27.2, 29.1, 29.2, 31.1, 32.1, 33.1, 33.2, 35.1, 35.2, 36.1, 36.2, 37.1, 38.1, 39.1, 40.1, 41.1, 42.1, 43.1, 44.1, 45.1, 46.1, 48.1, 49.1, 49.2, 50.1, 51.1, 52.2, 53.1, 54.1, 54.2, 55.2, 57.1, 58.1, 59.1, 60.1, 60.2, 61.1, 61.3, 62.1, 63.1, 63.3, 64.1, 65.1, 66.1, 67.1, 68.1, 69.1, 70.1, 70.2, 71.1, 72.1, 74.1, 75.1, 76.1, 77.1, 78.1, 81.2, 83.1, 85.1, 86.4, 87.1, 89.1, 90.1, 91.1, 93.1, 94.1, 95.1

Teacher's Manual:*

3, 19, 22, 31, 32, 33, 37, 45, 54, 56, 59, 64, 66, 67, 83, 86

COMPREHENSION
Understand and interpret information learned in a different form
Behavioral Terms Indicating Comprehension:

describe	generalize
reword	paraphrase
render	summarize
convert	translate
tell	infer
expand	outline
explain	project
specify	calculate

Sample Learning Outcomes (Student Edition):

Two essential art skills are keen observation and use of lines in drawing. Explain why these skills are so important.
(Lesson 1; page 231)

Explain the difference between tint and shade in color.
(Lesson 22; page 234)

Describe how to make a watercolor wash.
(Lesson 26; page 235)

Learning Outcomes Requiring Use of Comprehension:*

1.2, 1.3, 3.2, 4.4, 6.1, 6.2, 8.1, 9.1, 10.1, 12.1, 13.2, 14.3, 16.2, 19.2, 19.4, 20.1, 21.1, 21.2, 21.4, 23.2, 24.2, 25.2, 26.2, 26.5, 27.2, 28.1, 30.1, 31.3, 33.5, 34.1, 37.2, 39.4, 42.1, 43.3, 46.1, 47.1, 49.3, 50.2, 51.2, 51.3, 51.5, 52.1, 52.2, 53.2, 54.4, 55.1, 55.2, 56.1, 58.1, 58.2, 63.4, 69.2, 69.3, 70.4, 72.3, 73.1, 74.1, 74.5, 75.5, 78.2, 79.1, 80.1, 81.1, 81.5, 82.1, 83.3, 84.1, 86.1, 88.1, 90.2, 92.1, 94.1

Teacher's Manual:*

3, 4, 6, 8, 10, 13, 15, 23, 26, 27, 31, 32, 33, 42, 49, 51, 56, 57, 61, 66, 67, 75, 76, 84, 87, 93

Student Edition
*The first number of the *Learning Outcomes* represents the lesson number, the second refers to a specific question.
Teacher's Manual
**Numbers refer to lesson numbers. Thinking skills are found under "Planning Ahead" and "Helpful Teaching Hints."

Learning Outcomes
Correlated to Critical Thinking Skills

(Continued)

APPLICATION:
Use information learned to relate or apply ideas to new or unusual situations

Behavioral Terms Indicating Application:

apply	transfer
utilize	employ
change	manipulate
sketch	exercise
produce	develop
show	mobilize
dramatize	solve
demonstrate	relate

Sample Learning Outcomes (Student Edition):

Did you show gradual shading on the contours of three objects?
(Lesson 3; page 231)

Tell what you did to make your drawing of a hand look three-dimensional.
(Lesson 12; page 232)

Describe the features of Roman architecture you used in your building design.
(Lesson 70; page 241)

Learning Outcomes Requiring Use of Application:*

1.3, 2.2, 2.3, 3.3, 4.2, 5.2, 6.3, 6.4, 7.2, 7.5, 8.3, 8.4, 9.2, 10.3, 11.2, 12.2, 13.3, 14.2, 14.3, 16.3, 16.4, 17.2, 18.2, 19.3, 20.3, 31.3, 22.3, 23.2, 24.3, 25.3, 26.3, 27.3, 29.3, 30.2, 31.2, 32.2, 33.3, 34.2, 35.3, 36.3, 37.3, 38.2, 39.2, 40.2, 40.3, 42.2, 43.2, 44.2, 45.2, 46.2, 47.2, 48.2, 49.3, 49.4, 52.3, 53.3, 54.3, 55.3, 56.1, 57.2, 59.2, 60.3, 61.2, 62.2, 63.2, 64.2, 65.2, 66.2, 67.2, 68.3, 69.3, 70.3, 71.2, 72.2, 73.2, 74.2, 75.2, 76.2, 77.2, 79.2, 80.2, 83.2, 86.2, 88.2, 90.3, 92.2, 93.2, 94.2, 95.2

Teacher's Manual:**

1, 3, 7, 9, 14, 16, 21, 24, 26, 46, 51, 52, 53, 55, 56, 58, 59, 65, 69, 76, 82, 87, 93

ANALYSIS
Examine and break information down into its component parts and identify its unique characteristics

Behavioral Terms Indicating Analysis:

examine	separate
analyze	select
categorize	inspect
classify	scrutinize
simplify	survey
compare	search
diagram	experiment
dissect	illustrate

Sample Learning Outcomes (Student Edition):

Study the pictures by Burchfield and Hopper shown in this lesson. Compare and contrast the techniques these two artists used to create effective shadows in their pictures.
(Lesson 29; page 235)

In what ways are your abstract drawings and your realistic drawing still alike?
(Lesson 82; page 243)

How do Benton and Lee achieve a sense of movement in this lesson?
(Lesson 88; page 244)

Learning Outcomes Requiring Use of Analysis:*

2.2, 2.3, 3.5, 5.4, 6.5, 7.3, 7.4, 8.5, 10.5, 11.3, 12.4, 13.4, 14.4, 14.5, 15.5, 16.5, 17.4, 18.4, 19.5, 20.5, 22.5, 23.5, 25.5, 26.4, 26.5, 28.4, 29.5, 30.5, 32.3, 35.5, 36.4, 36.5, 43.5, 44.4, 47.4, 52.5, 56.5, 57.4, 58.5, 59.4, 60.5, 63.4, 64.4, 65.4, 66.4, 66.5, 69.5, 71.4, 73.3, 76.4, 80.4, 81.3, 82.3, 82.4, 84.5, 85.4, 87.3, 88.5, 92.4, 93.4, 94.3, 95.3

Teacher's Manual:**

4, 6, 11, 13, 34, 35, 50, 53, 54, 59, 62, 64, 66, 67, 69, 71, 77, 79, 80, 90, 92, 94

Student Edition
* The first number of the *Learning Outcomes* represents the lesson number, the second refers to a specific question.
Teacher's Manual
** Numbers refer to lesson numbers. Thinking skills are found under "Planning Ahead" and "Helpful Teaching Hints."

SYNTHESIS
Communicate, generate, or develop something new and original from what is learned

Behavioral Terms Indicating Synthesis:

unify	develop
combine	design
compose	originate
create	produce
form	generate
assemble	arrange
reorganize	invent
construct	imagine

Sample Learning Outcomes (Student Edition):

How did you transform the shapes and forms in your drawing into your own geometric design?
(Lesson 15; page 233)

Explain what you did to create a picture in an Oriental art style, including how you used line, space, and color.
(Lesson 31; page 235)

Tell how you created a center of interest for your collage.
(Lesson 38; page 237)

Learning Outcomes Requiring Use of Synthesis:*

3.4, 4.3, 5.3, 6.3, 8.3, 9.3, 10.4, 11.2, 12.3, 12.4, 14.2, 14.4, 15.3, 15.4, 16.3, 16.4, 17.3, 18.3, 20.4, 22.4, 23.4, 24.3, 24.4, 25.3, 25.4, 26.3, 26.4, 27.4, 28.1, 28.3, 29.4, 30.3, 30.4, 31.3, 33.4, 34.2, 35.4, 36.4, 37.4, 37.5, 38.3, 38.4, 39.3, 40.3, 41.2, 41.3, 42.3, 43.3, 43.4, 44.3, 44.4, 45.3, 46.3, 47.3, 48.3, 48.4, 50.3, 51.3, 51.4, 52.4, 53.4, 54.5, 55.4, 56.3, 56.4, 57.3, 58.3, 58.4, 59.3, 60.4, 61.4, 62.3, 64.3, 65.3, 66.3, 66.4, 67.3, 67.4, 68.4, 69.4, 70.4, 71.3, 72.3, 72.4, 73.3, 74.4, 75.3, 75.4, 76.3, 77.2, 77.3, 78.3, 79.3, 80.3, 81.4, 82.2, 83.3, 84.2, 84.3, 85.2, 85.3, 86.3, 87.2, 88.3, 88.4, 89.3, 90.4, 91.2, 91.3, 92.3, 93.3, 95.4

Teacher's Manual:**

4, 5, 7, 18, 20, 21, 35, 36, 51, 52, 55, 56, 57, 65, 72, 74, 75, 76, 78, 82, 83, 86, 91

EVALUATION
Make judgments and evaluate something based on either external or internal conditions or criteria

Behavioral Terms Indicating Evaluation:

evaluate	estimate
judge	measure
value	recommend
decide	assess
determine	criticize
rate	justify
appraise	grade
rank	discriminate

Sample Learning Outcomes (Student Edition):

Study Hiroshige's painting of *The Cat* shown in this lesson. How does he use space and line effectively in this composition?
(Lesson 28; page 235)

Express your feelings about how well you were able to show the personality of the person you modeled.
(Lesson 61; page 240)

Identify which of the three Mondrian paintings you like best, and explain why.
(Lesson 82; page 243)

Learning Outcomes Requiring Use of Evaluation:*

1.4, 2.4, 3.5, 4.4, 6.5, 7.4, 9.4, 11.3, 12.4, 13.4, 15.5, 16.5, 17.4, 18.4, 19.3, 20.5, 21.5, 22.5, 23.5, 24.5, 25.5, 26.5, 27.5, 31.4, 32.4, 33.5, 34.3, 34.4, 35.5, 37.5, 39.4, 40.4, 41.4, 42.4, 43.5, 44.5, 45.4, 46.4, 47.4, 48.5, 49.5, 50.4, 50.5, 52.5, 53.5, 55.5, 56.5, 58.5, 59.4, 60.5, 61.5, 62.4, 63.4, 67.5, 68.5, 70.5, 71.4, 72.5, 73.4, 77.4, 78.4, 79.4, 82.4, 83.5, 84.4, 85.4, 86.5, 87.4, 89.5, 90.5, 91.4, 92.5, 93.5, 94.4

Teacher's Manual:**

10, 11, 33, 37, 48, 53, 54, 62, 66, 70, 71, 75, 77, 79, 80, 83, 89

Student Edition
 *The first number of the *Learning Outcomes* represents the lesson number, the second refers to a specific question.
Teacher's Manual
**Numbers refer to lesson numbers. Thinking skills are found under "Planning Ahead" and "Helpful Teaching Hints."

Art Evaluation Record Sheet

Name: _____ Date: _____

Lesson Number: _____

Strand Identification (if used): _____

Instructions: Refer to the *Learning Outcomes* section (at the back of your book) which corresponds to the lesson you are evaluating. Use the blanks below to answer the questions listed for the lesson.

Understanding Art: _____

_____

_____

_____

_____

_____

_____

Creating Art: _____

_____

_____

_____

_____

_____

_____

_____

_____

_____

_____

Appreciating Art: _____

_____

_____

_____

_____

_____

_____

How to Do It: Art Media, Materials, and Techniques

A special section entitled *How to Do It* appears at the back of the Student Edition. The purpose of this section is to provide additional information on the use of art tools and materials, media, and techniques. It includes specific directions for how to do certain activities referred to in the lessons, such as mixing colors, preparing clay, or making papier-mâché. Key italicized words marked with asterisks within the lessons refer students to the *How to Do It* section for further information. In addition to providing more extensive coverage of methods, media, and art materials, large photographs and illustrations enhance visual learning of such processes. Safety precautions for hazardous tools or materials are also featured throughout the section where necessary.

Students and teachers are encouraged to become familiar with the contents of this section, not only for completing art lessons within the text, but also because the knowledge gained in this section enables students to improve their art skills and become more self-sufficient. The benefits for the teacher are also quite substantial. As students become more independent in referring to this section, they are less likely to depend on the teacher to provide the information for them.

The Glossary

Throughout the book, particular words and skills recur that students need to learn. Important words are identified in heavy type and are defined in the Glossary at the end of the Student Edition. All such words are defined in the text on the first occasion they are used. Since most students will do only a portion of the total number of lessons, they are also defined in the Glossary.

Artists' Reference and Index

A complete *Artists' Reference* and *Index* are included at the end of the Student Edition. The *Artists' Reference* provides a list of major artworks by master artists included in the book.

Book Strands

Book strands offer unique opportunities for individualization of art education to occur. There are fourteen book strands identified by names such as

"Exploring with Paint" and "Fantasy and Distortion." Students will enjoy being able to choose a strand with a title they find interesting. Likewise, students will appreciate being able to identify those other lessons that have themes and concepts relevant to a lesson they particularly enjoyed. In anticipation of this desire, each lesson outline in this teacher's edition is followed by a book strand that includes the lesson. This makes it easy for you to direct interested students on a course of study they will enjoy.

Following is a short description of each book strand, including the philosophy behind its conception. Using the book strands is just like using the unit strands; see pages V and VI for these instructions.

Strand 1: Exploring with Paint
Step One of this strand consists of two lessons that ask students to choose between working in transparent watercolor and working in opaque tempera. This leads to a choice in Step Two between the technical exploration of the dry brush technique and a study of the influential painting styles of Van Gogh, Gauguin, and Cézanne. The strand ends with students being able to choose from among three very different painting lessons: tempera batik technique, a descriptive picture from memory, or a painting inspired by a poem.

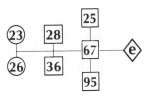

Strand 2: Creating with Lines
The strand opens with lessons requiring students to study lines that describe contours. At Step Two the students may work with lines to create woven textiles, wire sculpture, or architectural skeletons. The concept of line is further expanded in Step Three to include options in macramé, lettering, and sculpture made from string.

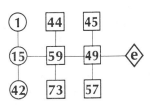

Strand 3: Designing with Shapes and Objects

The first choice involves collage lessons using cloth and paper. A more complex collage is included in Step Two, together with lesson choices on block printing and modular sculpture. Step Three extends these topics with lessons on imaginative lettering, designing a poster, and carving simple sculptural planes.

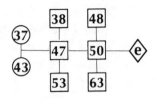

Strand 4: Surfaces and Textures

Step One consists of two lessons that introduce textures in contrasting ways—with stitchery and with ceramics. The study of textures continues in Step Two with lessons on weaving, modeling, and carving. Step Three consists of choices that include bead arrangements, embossed foils, and decorated pottery surfaces.

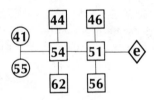

Strand 5: Contrast and Opposites

The choices in Step One require students to draw objects that show gradual and rapid changes from light to dark, and include a lesson on mirror images. Step Two includes three very different approaches to the topic. One lesson asks students to depict old and young people. Another lesson concentrates on changing realistic objects into abstract shapes. Finally, one lesson stresses the contrasts to be observed between night and day. Two unusual lessons conclude the strand. The first instructs students on how to draw a picture to look like a photographic negative. The second asks students to show people and pets who look alike.

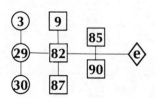

Strand 6: Near and Far

The strand opens with two drawing lessons in which students either produce shading with dots or practice the observation of details. The Step Two lessons are about drawing in perspective, either from normal positions or from the viewpoint of a bird. The strand ends with choices among lessons about using atmospheric perspective or about the techniques involved in drawing buildings.

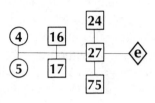

Strand 7: Objects and Places

One of the choices in Step One is for those who need help studying contours, while the others ask for drawings of plants, rocks, and animals. Step Two consists of lessons designed to help sharpen students' visual memories. In Step Three, students may use what they have learned earlier in the strand to solve one of three very different landscape problems.

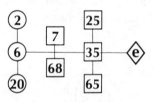

Strand 8: Buildings and Bridges

Since Greek and Roman architecture still influence the design of buildings today, it is appropriate that this strand should open with lessons on these two styles. Step Two introduces architectural styles from the Middle Ages and from Mexico—both of which continue to influence our architecture. The strand ends with assignments to make original designs for bridges and buildings.

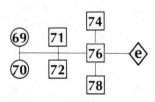

Strand 9: Artistic Messages

Step One asks students to choose between assignments based on either silhouettes or rhythmic brush strokes. The choices at Step Two give opportunities for communicating through distortion, fantasy, or verbal description. The strand ends with lessons in which students may convey a social message, a feeling of peacefulness, or the image of a hero.

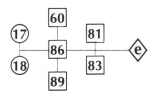

Strand 10: Visions and Feelings
For special effects, artists frequently show unusual views of places in their art. The first step in this strand gives students two opportunities to think about interesting viewpoints. In Step Two, the students may express their ideas through sculpture, creations derived from microscope slides, or robot-like constructions. The strand ends with students creating original art based on ideas that emphasize various forms of distortion.

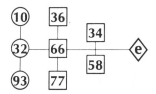

Strand 11: Learning from Artists
Step One introduces students to the benefits derived from studying the work of professional artists. At this point, students choose to study great figures from the Renaissance or the founders of the contemporary art world. At the next step, choices are between American architecture and painting. The strand ends with lessons based on selections from 20th-century American painting and sculpture.

Strand 12: Studying People
People occupy a central place in the study of art, and

students begin this strand by drawing either a portrait or a full figure. Step Two expands students' experience in drawing the body by having them draw hands or create model heads out of clay. The strand ends with more complex drawing and modeling assignments.

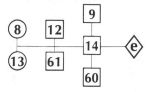

Strand 13: Fantasy and Distortion
Almost all artists use their imaginations to alter the shapes of objects and make them more interesting or exciting. For this reason, this strand begins with two lessons on distorting shapes. Three choices are given at Step Two that encourage students to explore caricature, dream imagery, or rhythmic distortion. The first step is designed to encourage students to attempt extreme forms of fantasy and distortion.

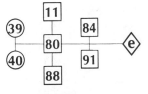

Strand 14: The Road to Abstraction
Step One lets students choose among drawing, painting, and relief assemblage. While each lesson is different, each one provides students with opportunities to begin thinking and working abstractly. The Step Two choices direct students to study abstractions in carving and painting. The strand ends with lessons that ask students to take advantage of learning from the work of two of the most important abstract artists of the 20th century.

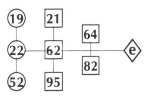

Strand 15: Learning About Shape
This strand focuses on shape as a two-dimensional

design element created with various media. Step One includes the choice of creating simple cloth shapes or geometric abstract shapes. Lessons in calligraphy or silhouette painting in Step Two define the meaning of shape further. Finally, the student may choose to continue working with shape as an abstraction of reality or discover the effect of taking shape into the three-dimensional world of mobiles.

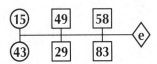

Strand 16: Form as Illusion and Reality
Steps One and Two of this strand offer the student the opportunity to create the illusion of three-dimensional form in the two-dimensional realm by shading objects or the human figure. Step Three includes lessons on three-dimensional forms either in sculpture or architecture.

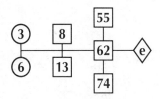

Strand 17: Relationships in Design
Step One of this strand introduces the student to proportion in the human figure. In Step Two the importance of proportion in creating varied yet balanced artwork is studied in either calligraphy or clay modeling. The final step allows the student to develop an awareness of movement or distortion in proportion.

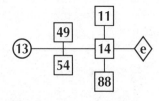

Strand 18: Famous Styles and Artists
Step One of this strand invites the student to choose a lesson from three very different art styles. In the second step three art styles leading to present modern art are offered as choices. Step Three provides an opportunity for in-depth study of famous artists.

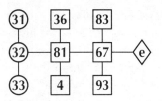

Strand 19: Movement in Art
This strand explores the importance of successfully moving the viewer's eye through, and keeping it focused within, a piece of artwork. The lesson in Step One introduces the student to this path of vision principle. Step Two allows for further practice in two-dimensional projects. Finally, the principle is applied to three-dimensional artwork in a choice of sculpture lessons.

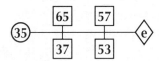

Strand 20: Rhythmic Repetition
In Step One of this strand, rhythm, the regular repetition of any single design element, is practiced in combination with the other principles of art. Step Two offers the students two activities in which rhythm is created primarily with line. The last step provides choices in learning more about rhythm through either printed patterns, cut-out shapes, or architectural lines and forms.

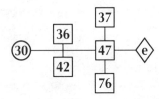

Applying the Strand Concept

As you can see, book strands and unit strands offer remarkable individualization possibilities. However, because of the immaturity or inexperience of their students, teachers may think it wise to restrict student choices to a few strands. Occasionally, though, a class may be mature enough to be given the freedom to select any strand—unit or book—and choose any pathway through it. In fact, the experience gained during the two years of field testing through which these books originally went indicates that a larger proportion of students than would have been thought possible respond favorably to being responsible for their own education in this way. Furthermore, experience shows that, with a curriculum based on individualization, students who work slowly no longer experience pressure to keep pace with other students in the class, while the faster and generally more capable students are not frustrated by having to wait for the rest of the class to complete an assignment. Another outcome of full individualization, unexpected but desirable, is that the quantity of tools and materials needed to operate an art program declines considerably because of the dispersal of need and the variable speed of student production. Teachers should realize one thing about full individualization, however. With such a program it becomes necessary to maintain some form of written evaluation with the students in order to make record-keeping manage-able. An example of such an evaluation form is depicted on page xii, but teachers should choose any format with which they are comfortable.

Postscript

The remainder of this Teacher's Edition provides useful information about the units and the lessons that make up the units, together with ideas and book references for enriching and supplementing instruction. A scope and sequence chart and a supplies chart showing art materials needed throughout the course are also included.

Art In Action: Scope and Sequence (Second Course)

I. Elements of Art

Line	5-9, 12, 14, 15, 17, 19-21, 28, 32, 33, 36-39, 41-46, 65, 67-69, 71, 79, 96, 97, 99, 108, 109, 111, 114, 130, 131, 134, 135, 144, 150, 152, 155, 178, 181, 184, 188, 189, 191, 206, 216
Shape	18, 19, 21, 28, 29, 34, 35, 46, 51, 52, 53, 66-70, 74-77, 86-89, 96-99, 107-111, 114, 119-123, 127, 131-135, 139, 141, 144, 146, 152, 175, 188-191, 196, 201, 216
Form	5, 10, 11, 18, 28, 29, 31, 34, 44, 50, 67, 70, 82, 86, 117, 120, 126, 127, 130, 135, 140-141, 142-143, 144-145, 178, 196, 211
Space	5, 28, 29, 70, 71, 79, 89, 93, 111, 130, 131, 134, 135, 144, 145, 149, 178
Texture	10, 16, 17, 19, 28, 29, 34, 41, 44, 46, 64, 65, 73, 89, 95, 98-101, 106, 117, 119, 126, 129, 136-142, 144, 150, 188, 196, 205
Color	5, 12, 13, 22, 35, 49-83, 86, 87, 89, 94-95, 96-97, 98-99, 101, 106, 112, 114, 115, 150-151, 152-153, 181, 182-183, 184-185, 186-187, 188-189, 190, 198, 199, 216, 217
Value	10, 11, 13, 21, 41, 52, 53, 54, 55, 59, 60, 62, 69, 70

II. Principles of Art

Balance	5, 52, 53, 57, 60, 63, 66, 68-70, 79, 120, 121, 132-135, 137, 150, 167, 173, 194
Variety	5, 26, 35, 65, 86, 88, 89, 94, 95, 96, 98, 107, 121, 132
Rhythm	5, 69, 80, 82, 86, 87, 107, 181, 189, 201
Movement	5, 32, 33, 38, 64, 65, 70, 71, 74, 79, 80, 81, 82, 87, 122, 130, 132, 133, 145, 154, 184, 200, 201
Emphasis	5, 20, 25, 26-27, 32, 33, 40, 41, 65, 69, 78, 87, 89, 138, 140, 145, 184, 185, 189, 190, 191, 200
Proportion	5, 20-21, 22-23, 28-29, 30-31, 33, 46, 47, 111, 124, 125, 144, 200, 201
Unity	5, 33, 51, 53, 66, 69, 75, 79, 89, 97, 99, 109, 112, 114, 121, 123, 142, 144, 146, 149, 184, 191, 194

III. Creative Expression Using Various Media and Materials

Drawing: pencil	7, 9, 11, 13, 15, 17, 19, 21, 23, 25, 27, 29, 31, 33, 35, 37, 39, 41, 43, 46, 51, 53, 55, 57, 59, 63, 65, 67, 69, 71, 73, 75, 77, 79, 82, 89, 91, 93, 107, 109, 111, 114, 119, 143, 151, 153, 155, 157, 161, 163, 165, 167, 169, 171, 173, 175, 178, 185, 187, 189, 195, 197, 199, 201, 203, 211, 213, 216
charcoal	25, 33, 171, 211
ink	7, 13, 25, 27, 43, 71, 109, 111, 171, 173, 178, 213
chalk	25, 46, 59, 95
crayon	33, 35, 43, 46, 197, 199
oil pastel	35, 43, 46, 151, 155, 157, 161, 163, 165, 171, 175, 178, 183, 199, 213
colored marker	7, 13, 35, 59, 109, 114, 151, 155, 157, 159, 161, 163, 165, 173, 178, 185, 197, 199
colored pencils	37, 151, 155, 159, 161, 163, 165, 171, 175, 178
Painting: watercolor	60, 61, 62, 63, 65, 65, 67, 69, 71
tempera	51, 53, 55, 57, 59, 64, 65, 67, 69
other	73, 75, 77, 79, 82, 109, 114, 121, 151, 153, 155, 157, 159, 161, 163, 165, 173, 175, 183, 185, 187, 197, 199, 205, 207, 209, 211, 213, 216
Printmaking	106, 107, 223
Sculpture modeling	117, 124-125, 126-127, 128-129, 136-137, 138-139, 159, 161, 166-173, 175, 178, 205, 207, 209, 211
carving	117, 140, 141, 142, 143, 144, 145, 146, 147

VII. Related Subject Areas (Cont'd)	
Mathematics	34, 35, 51-53, 96, 97, 132, 133
Science	12, 16, 44, 46, 47, 72, 196, 197, 198, 202, 203, 210
Music	18, 49, 214, 216
Industrial Arts	14, 35, 179, 202, 203
Creative Arts	36, 66, 110-115, 209, 214, 215, 216, 217

VIII. Aesthetic Valuing Using Critical Thinking Skills

Knowledge	5, 6, 8, 10, 11, 12, 14, 16, 20, 22, 24, 26, 28, 30-32, 34, 36, 38, 40, 42, 44, 47, 49, 50, 52, 54, 56, 58, 60, 62-64, 66-68, 70-74, 76-78, 80-83, 86-88, 90, 92, 94, 96, 98, 100, 102, 104, 106, 108, 110, 112, 117, 118, 120, 122, 124, 126, 127, 128, 130, 132, 134, 136, 138, 140, 142, 144, 145, 147, 149, 150, 152, 154, 156, 158-160, 162, 164, 166, 168, 170, 172, 174, 176, 178, 181, 182, 184, 186-188, 190-192, 194, 196, 200, 202, 204, 206, 208-210, 212, 214, 217
Comprehension	5-8, 10, 12, 14, 18, 19, 21-24, 27, 28, 31, 32, 34, 38-42, 44, 49, 50, 54, 56, 62, 64, 66, 70, 74, 76, 79, 81, 82, 83, 88, 96, 98, 102, 104, 106, 108, 114, 117, 120, 122, 124, 126, 127, 128, 135, 136, 140, 141, 144, 145, 149-152, 154, 156, 158, 160, 163, 170, 178, 182, 184, 185, 187, 191, 192, 193, 197, 198, 200-202, 206, 209, 211, 212, 214, 217
Application	5, 6, 7, 9, 11, 13, 14, 16, 17, 18, 19, 21, 25, 29, 33, 35, 37, 39, 46, 47, 51, 53, 55, 59, 61, 63, 65, 73, 79, 82, 87, 91, 93, 95, 97, 99, 101, 107, 111, 114, 119, 121, 123, 125, 127, 129, 131, 133, 135, 137, 139, 141, 143, 151, 155, 157, 159, 161, 163, 167, 169, 173, 187, 189, 191, 195, 199, 201, 204, 205, 207, 211
Analysis	7-9, 11, 14-23, 25, 27, 29, 31, 32, 34, 35, 38, 39, 42, 43, 44, 46, 51, 53, 65, 67, 71-73, 78, 79, 83, 88, 93, 95, 97, 103, 114, 115, 117, 121, 122, 123, 124, 126, 129, 131, 134, 136, 138-143, 146, 147, 151-153, 155, 161, 163, 165, 169, 170, 171, 176, 178, 179, 182-187, 189, 191, 193, 194, 197, 199, 200, 204, 206, 207, 211, 216
Synthesis	5-7, 9, 11, 13, 15, 17, 19, 21, 23, 25, 27, 29, 31, 33, 35, 37, 39, 41-43, 46, 47, 51, 53, 55, 57, 59, 61, 63, 65, 67, 69, 71, 73, 75, 77, 79, 82, 87, 89, 91, 93, 95, 97, 99, 100, 103, 105, 107, 109, 111, 114, 115, 119, 121, 123, 125, 127, 129, 131, 133, 135, 137, 139, 141, 143, 146, 147, 153, 155, 157, 159, 161, 163, 165, 167, 169, 171, 173, 175, 178, 179, 181, 183, 185, 187, 189, 191, 193, 195, 197, 199, 201, 203, 205, 207, 209, 211, 216, 217
Evaluation	7, 11, 15-17, 19, 20, 25, 27, 31, 33, 35, 38, 39, 41, 43, 45-47, 51, 53, 54, 57, 61, 70, 77, 79, 81, 82, 83, 86, 87, 93, 98, 101, 106, 107, 109, 111, 112, 114, 120, 121, 123, 126, 131, 135, 140, 141, 150, 155, 159, 163, 165, 171, 173, 176, 179, 181, 186, 187, 197, 207, 208, 213, 216, 217, 231-245

Unit I
Line, Tone, and Value

Learning Objectives

In this unit, the students will achieve the following objectives:

Understanding Art

- Understand the important roles of observation and visual memory in the creation of art
- Understand how to use different drawing tools to achieve the required effects

Creating Art

- Use a variety of line and shading techniques
- Accurately depict three-dimensional objects
- Achieve perspective in drawings
- Draw the human body in correct proportion
- Use geometric shapes in compositions

Appreciating Art

- Notice the elements of design in everyday objects
- Study different drawing styles of well-known artists, appreciating each as valid
- Appreciate the amount of work and study required beforehand to draw accurately

Unit Strands

A strand consists of a group of related lessons where the student is expected to begin with one of the lesson choices available on the far left (arranged vertically), complete it, proceed horizontally to the next group of choices, make a choice and complete the lesson, and so forth, until the entire sequence has been completed. (See page vii for complete instructions on using strands.) The unit strands for this unit are diagramed at the top of the next column.

Strand A: Lines, Shapes, and Details

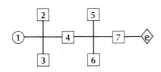

Strand B: Drawing People

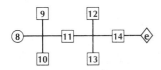

Strand C: Drawing Styles and Techniques

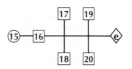

Background Information

This unit develops basic drawing skills, building on those the students may already have. Emphasis is on translating close observation of the world around us into drawings that use a variety of line and shading techniques. On completion of these lessons, students will have learned how to manipulate a variety of media, using techniques mastered by well-known artists. They will have learned the basic principles of perspective drawing, the proportions of the human figure, and how to design compositions based on geometric forms.

Lesson 1, Contour Drawing, and Lesson 2, Outside and Inside Shapes, introduce students to inner and outer contour drawing. Emphasis is on accurate observation and the development of the visual, mental, and manual connections essential to mastering drawing skills. By focusing attention on both inner and outer contours of objects, these lessons help students to begin developing sensitivity to three-dimensional forms.

Lesson 3 and Lesson 4 then require students to demonstrate awareness of three-dimensionality, as these lessons teach students how to shade drawings of round objects. The students use gradation of dark and light values to indicate tone. Such shading skills will be useful to the students as they attempt later lessons on drawing the human figure.

Lesson 5, Drawing Details and Close-ups, and Lesson 6, Sketching and Drawing Natural Objects, again place the emphasis on close attention to details—for these lessons, the realistic details of man-made and natural objects. Lesson 5 focuses on rendering by line alone, a technique common to much current graphic art, while Lesson 6 encourages students to incorporate texture into their drawings.

Lesson 7 places a new stress on observation. It trains the students to develop the kind of observational skills that lead to visual memory. The students are asked to use their memories when drawing, as a means of pointing out that observation must be conscious.

Lesson 8, A Three-Quarter View Portrait, and Lesson 9, Old and Young People, introduce students to portraiture. In Lesson 8, students learn the correct proportions of the human head and how to render a three-quarter profile. Line and shading techniques learned in prior lessons are incorporated in the portrait. In Lesson 9, skills learned are expanded as students are asked to create a double portrait of an older and a younger person. Students are required to observe closely the differences in the faces in order to render them realistically.

Lesson 10, Sketching in the Style of Leonardo da Vinci, helps the students to develop a creative approach to line drawing and shading techniques, by asking them to emulate Leonardo da Vinci's style. Each student is encouraged to make rough sketches and choose one to refine in a finished drawing, deciding on the most appropriate medium to use. This lesson thus requires students to develop evaluative and critical skills about their own work in relation to that of a master artist.

Lesson 11, Exaggerated Drawings and Caricatures, also helps students to explore a more creative drawing style, this time by focusing on distortion. Satirical caricatures and political cartoons are introduced as legitimate art forms having a long history in Western culture.

Lesson 12, Portrait of Hands, and Lesson 13, Human Measurements, continue the focus on drawing the human figure. Lesson 12 requires the students to study the proportions of the hand and to concentrate on rendering its gestures accurately, using line and shading. Lesson 13 teaches the proportions of the body and the ratio of one part to another, and it requires a full-figure drawing.

Lesson 14, People in Action, asks the students to use skills learned in the previous figure drawing lessons. They must apply these skills to the sophisticated task of drawing the human figure in action.

Lesson 15, Geometric Shapes, provides a transition between the freer approach to figure drawing and the more prescriptive requirements of perspective drawing. The lesson calls for precision in the use of graphic tools and asks students to analyze various abstract compositions.

Lesson 16, Showing Depth and Distance, and Lesson 17, Bird's-Eye View, involve perspective drawing. Lesson 16 introduces the basics, teaching the students how to determine the horizon line and the vanishing point and how to draw in true perspective. Lesson 17 requires the students to use their knowledge of perspective to create drawings in which the vanishing point falls below eye level.

Lesson 18 invites the students to use the skills they have learned so far in the unit to create distorted views of objects or scenes. Imagination and creativity are required as the students create pencil drawings.

Lesson 19, Different Styles of Drawing, asks the students to explore the different drawing styles of well-known artists, and practice to see if they can achieve similar effects. Students must make conscious choices involving the styles and media they want to try.

Lesson 20 has the students draw animals, preferably from life, starting with rough sketches and proceeding to a finished drawing. Students are asked to closely observe structure, form, proportion, and movement of animals, and the texture of fur, feathers, skin, or shell, to create realistic drawings in the media of their choice.

Strategies for Motivation

Good observational skills are transferable to the creation of all art forms. Therefore, it is wise to make observation an ongoing, conscious element of your students' classroom experience. You can do this by emphasizing the details of objects to be drawn and by increasing the students' interest in the subjects to be drawn. Following are some suggestions along these lines, but you should refer to individual lesson guides for specific applications.

- Outline the objects to be drawn with colored yarn or twine.
- Use flood lamps to highlight the light and dark values of rounded objects.
- Use automobile parts or interesting machine parts when setting up still lifes.
- Use photographs of your local community for lessons on perspective.
- Ask a local athlete to model for action poses.
- Invite a mime or ballet dancer to perform, serving as inspiration for lessons on depicting hands and on figure drawing.
- Invite grandparents of students, or distinguished older persons from the community, to pose for portraiture lessons.

Extending Art
Exploring Art

The Exploring Art feature in Unit I sensitizes students

to art in nature and the environment by directing them to make a series of quick sketches of a live animal. The student text contains examples by Leonardo da Vinci. Have on hand additional animal drawings and paintings by a variety of other artists (Albrecht Dürer, John James Audubon, Frederic Remington, Henri Rousseau, Marc Chagall, Franz Ernst, Pablo Picasso, Henri Matisse). Suggestions for further extending this lesson follow.

- Arrange a field trip to a local zoo. Instruct the students to take their sketchbooks, choose one or two animals to concentrate on, and make at least five quick sketches of each. Students can use these sketches as the bases for later drawings.
- Provide a series of drawings illustrating how animated cartoons work. Then encourage students to make their own sets of sketches for animation. Sketches (a minimum of ten) can be bound into a booklet; quickly flipping the pages provides the illusion of motion.

Additional Activities

A number of lessons in this unit may be extended in ways that enhance their creative and teaching potential and provide additional motivational stimuli to the students. Although the individual lesson guides provide specific suggestions, here are some general activities that you may wish to include in your program:

- Arrange for the students to visit a retirement home where they can get to know members and sketch them.
- Visit local art museums and galleries which have exhibits relating to current lessons.
- Ask each student to draw his or her own street for perspective lessons.

Evaluating Procedures

As noted in the introduction to this book, evaluation in art classes poses unique problems for the teacher. (See pages vi–vii.) The Learning Outcomes address the need for self-evaluation and test the students on the details of what they have learned. However, the teacher still needs some means of determining the extent of a student's application of specifics to a solid core of basic art knowledge. Three things are involved in this type of evaluation:

1. A written test of the student's recall of important facts
2. An examination of the student's artwork in terms of the achievement of certain previously stated goals

3. An oral discussion with the student involving his or her comments on a particular piece of art

These three evaluative components for Unit I are explained below.

Vocabulary

Students who complete this unit should be able to define and correctly use the art terms listed below. A written test on the unit should, then, be based on these terms.

abstract	modified contour
blind contour drawing	drawing
caricature	perspective
center of interest	pointillism
compass	portrait
contours	profile
converge	proportions
cross-hatching	protractor
depth	ratios
distort	render
eye level	shading
freehand	solidity
geometric	symmetrical
gesture	texture
gradation	three-dimensional
graphic design	tone
horizon	values
horizontal	vanishing point
hues	vertical
images	visual memory
internal contours	visuals
iris	wash
medium	

Skills

The artworks students create in this unit should meet the standards listed below. Be certain that the students are aware of these standards both as they plan and as they work. You may choose to keep this list posted throughout the time spent on this unit.

- Drawings reveal close observation, showing awareness of specific parts, spaces, and contours, and accurately portraying distinctive details.
- A variety of lines is used for different effects.
- Perspective is accurately depicted through proper shading techniques.
- Correct body proportions are used.

Application of Knowledge

Listening to a student talk about an artwork can give you a true sense of how much the student

3

understands the basic elements and principles of design. However, the planning behind such a discussion is important. First, the work to be discussed must be chosen in advance and studied by the teacher. Questions must be written that will lead the student into the correct areas of emphasis. Last, the discussion should be arranged to take place on a one-to-one basis so that the more reticent students are not left out of a group discussion.

A suggested artwork to use for discussion purposes in this unit is any of the works by David Ramos which depict people, such as *The Warrior* or *The Sand Bucket*.

Supplementary Materials and Resources

Teacher Resources

de Fiore, Gaspare. *Learning to Draw.* Volume 1 of *The Drawing Course.* New York: Watson-Guptill Publications, 1983.
This book emphasizes learning to draw by studying and emulating the old masters, of whose works numerous examples are given. Covered are learning to see, drawing from life, composition, color theory, and geometric design. This is an excellent how-to resource book that also functions to give art history background.

Educational Motion Pictures 1980 Catalog. Bloomington: Indiana University Audio Visual Center.
This catalog lists available films and gives brief descriptions of each. Recommended listings are *Drawings of da Vinci* and *Drawing with Pencil.*

Hogarth, Burne. *Dynamic Figure Drawing.* New York: Watson-Guptill Publications, 1976.
This book stresses drawing the figure in action. It shows how the body is composed of round forms and planes.

Mendelowitz, Daniel M. *Drawing* and *A Study Guide.* New York: Holt, Rinehart, and Winston, Inc., 1967.
Drawing discusses the history of drawing from cave drawings to 20th-century Expressionism, covering line, form, value, texture, media, and imagination. Numerous reproductions illustrate the discussions. The supplementary study guide provides a number of self-instruction activities suitable for classrooms.

Nicolaides, Kimon. *The Natural Way to Draw.* Boston: Houghton Mifflin Co., 1969.
This book covers contour drawing, gesture, modeling of the human figure, animal drawing, memory drawing, quick sketching, and drawing in ink. It is illustrated with reproductions of artworks by master artists: Rodin, Michelangelo, Rembrandt, Goya, etc.

Richter, Jean Paul, ed. *The Notebooks of Leonardo da Vinci.* 2 vols. New York: Dover Publications, Inc., 1970.
Compiled from the original manuscripts, the *Notebooks* contain numerous drawings, including pictures of Leonardo da Vinci's inventions, and his notes and thoughts.

Simon, Howard. *Techniques of Drawing.* New York: Dover Publications, Inc., 1963.
This book gives problems and examples to solve concerning line, form, movement, use of perspective, outdoor sketching, and drawing animals. Techniques and use of media are presented, with ample examples by the author and well-known artists illustrating them.

Zappalorti, Robert. *Drawing Sharp Focus Still Lifes.* New York: Watson-Guptill Publications, 1981.
Including discussions on perspective, proportion, rendering, and use of materials, this book shows how to draw all types of objects. Illustrations are by the author.

Student Resources

Blegvad, Erik. *Self-Portrait: Erik Blegvad.* Reading, Massachusetts: Addison-Wesley Publishing Co., Inc., 1979.
This is the second in a series of first-person picture books by distinguished authors. Danish-born Blegvad illustrated *The Borrowers* and many other children's books. Here, he tells how he became an artist and shows examples of the work he does. The book is illustrated with black-and-white pen drawings and watercolors.

Hyman, Trina Schart. *Self-Portrait: Trina Schart Hyman.* Reading, Massachusetts: Addison-Wesley Publishing Co., Inc., 1981.
This book is third in the above series. Trina Schart Hyman tells about how she became interested in art as a child, her art school training, and her work as the

illustrator of *Snow White* and *Sleeping Beauty.* Colored illustrations are included.

Laliberté, Norman and Alex Mogelon. *Drawing with Pencils.* New York: Van Nostrand Reinhold Co., 1969.
This is a whimsical, inventive book showing how to use the pencil imaginatively. It includes demonstrations; projects to do; instructions on how to use rubbings, textures, oil pastels, and colored pencils in artworks; and a section on creating collages and cutouts. (Laliberté is famous for his banner designs.) This book shows students that art is fun.

Raboff, Ernest. *Leonardo da Vinci.* Garden City, NY: Doubleday and Co., 1978.
One of a series which includes books about Michelangelo, Raphael, Picasso, Rembrandt, etc., this book includes information about Leonardo da Vinci—his works and his style. Presented in a colorful and vibrant way, the series is an excellent way to introduce art history to students.

TEACHING SUGGESTIONS for Lessons 1–20

LESSON 1

Contour Drawing

Suggested Art Materials

See the art materials list for this lesson in the student book.

Planning Ahead

Introduce the concept of contours by having the students run their hands along the contours of objects. (Choose items that have interesting shapes, such as roller skates, a coffee grinder, a bird cage.)
Additional Materials Needed:
objects with interesting shapes

Helpful Teaching Hints

- Project the silhouettes of objects by placing them on an overhead projector. Have the students draw the outlines of the objects.*
- Use drawings by Matisse and Picasso as examples of contour drawing.**
Additional Materials Needed:
  *overhead projector
**drawings by Matisse and Picasso

Book Strand

Book strand 2, Creating with Lines, includes this lesson in its diagram, pictured below. See page xiii for a complete description of this strand.

Creating with Lines

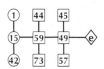

LESSON 2

Outside and Inside Shapes

Suggested Art Materials

See the art materials list in the student book.

Planning Ahead

Collect numerous objects that have simple but interesting shapes (transparent bottles, vases, wooden toys) for wrapping with string.

Helpful Teaching Hints

- Try suspending the objects or standing them at unusual angles to add interest to the lesson.
- Before wrapping the objects with string, ask students to study the objects from different angles. Have them trace the external contours with their fingers, noting how those contours change from different viewpoints.
- When the students wrap the thick string around the selected object, point out that the string should not completely cover the object.
- Discuss how drawing the string as it follows the form of an object is a method of creating the volume, or internal contours, of the object. To help students understand this concept, have them visualize the object as made up of a series of coils (as in pottery) stacked on top of each other.
- The lines of the string function as the basis for shading areas in the final drawing. Review the various shading techniques on page 219 in the student edition.

Book Strand

Book strand 7, Objects and Places, includes this lesson in its diagram, pictured below. See page xiv for a complete description of this strand.

Objects and Places

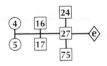

LESSON 3

Shading Rounded Surfaces

Suggested Art Materials

See the art materials list in the student book.

Helpful Teaching Hints

- Define *gradation* as a gradual change from light to dark. Place a number of white, rounded objects against a dark background. Cast a flood lamp on the arrangement, moving the light around to show how values shift.*
- Demonstrate a number of shading techniques, including cross-hatching.
- Show drawings by Leonardo da Vinci, Thomas Nast, and Raphael as examples of shading.**

Additional Materials Needed:
  *white, rounded objects; dark cloth for background; flood lamp
  **drawings by Leonardo da Vinci, Thomas Nast, Raphael

Book Strands

Book strand 5, Contrast and Opposites, and book strand 16, Form as Illusion and Reality, include this lesson in their diagrams, pictured below. See pages xiv and xvi for a complete description of these strands.

Contrast and Opposites   Form as Illusion and Reality

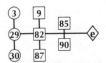   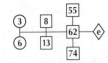

LESSON 4

Dots ... Dots ... Dots

Suggested Art Materials

See the art materials list for this lesson in the student book.

Planning Ahead

Collect photographs from newspapers and maga-

zines to illustrate the use of dots (actually screens) in photo reproduction. Have magnifying glasses available for students to use when viewing the photographs.
Additional Materials Needed:
magazine and newspaper photographs, magnifying glasses

Helpful Teaching Hints

- Point out that this technique is another way of shading, of creating value differences to make objects appear three-dimensional.
- Show reproductions of artworks by Andy Warhol and other Pop artists (who used this technique). Contrast these works with those by Georges Seurat.*
- As an extension of this lesson, have the students do a second drawing, this time using color.
Additional Materials Needed:
*artworks by Pop artists and by Seurat

Book Strand

Book strand 6, Near and Far, includes this lesson in its diagram, pictured below. See page xiv for a complete description of this strand.

Near and Far

LESSON 5

Drawing Details and Close-ups

Suggested Art Materials

See the art materials list for this lesson in the student book.

Planning Ahead

Collect interesting man-made objects (shoes, tools, kitchen utensils, etc.) and line drawings (from newspaper, magazine, or catalog advertisements) that represent these same items, to show how graphic artists render objects.
Additional Materials Needed:
objects, illustrations of them

Helpful Teaching Hints

- Invite a graphic artist to demonstrate for your class how he or she draws an object.

- Have the students draw imaginary machines or utensils in detail and write complete explanations about how the "inventions" work.

Related Art Career (graphic designer)

The job titles graphic designer and graphic artist are generally used interchangeably, although graphic artists often work in the fields of printmaking only. The graphic designer, one who creates and executes plans for a project, is the planner of the printed page. The designer organizes the type, lettering, and visuals in a layout and selects ink, paper, and printing processes to be used to create the total image. The projects can range from books, magazines, packages, posters, signs, advertisements and trademarks to the newer multi-media fields of computer graphics, film strips, slides, and tapes. A good art and design program will prepare the designer to work with a variety of media and materials, including photography, typeface, manuscripts, silk screen, and lettering.

Ask students to bring in the entire local newspaper. Have them identify the various kinds of artists and designers needed in the production of the newspaper. Discuss differences in style, use of media, or training required for each. Also have them look in the classified ad section for related art career opportunities.

Book Strand

Book strand 6, Near and Far, includes this lesson in its diagram, pictured below. See page xiv for a complete description of this strand.

Near and Far

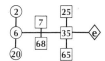

LESSON 6

Sketching and Drawing Natural Objects

Suggested Art Materials

See the art materials list for this lesson in the student book.

Planning Ahead

Ask the students a week in advance to begin making sketches of natural objects in their environment. Have them each choose a favorite sketch and bring it, along with the object it represents, to class for discussion.

Helpful Teaching Hints

- Point out that the portrayal of texture in a drawing is a way of showing the form or solidity of an object.
- Contrast the following man-made objects with natural objects of similar shapes: a pointed seashell (contrast with a top or a Christmas tree ornament), a large sunflower head (contrast with a flying disc or a hubcap), a pumpkin (contrast with a basketball).*

Additional Materials Needed:
*natural and man-made objects with similar shapes

Related Art Career (scientific illustrator)

The job of illustrator is usually defined more specifically by the area being illustrated. Many illustrators, for example, specialize in a certain field, such as sports, fashions, comics, technical or scientific illustration.

John Audubon, founder of the Audubon Society, is one of the most well-known scientific illustrators. He used keen observation methods, similar to those of Leonardo da Vinci, to examine the minute details of nature in order to create photographically accurate records of wildlife.

Today the photographer is replacing the illustrator in many areas. Have students bring in science textbooks and scientific or medical publications from the library. Ask them to identify and compare the use of these two art forms in illustrations.

Book Strands

Book strand 7, Objects and Places, and book strand 16, Form as Illusion and Reality, include this lesson in their diagrams, pictured below. See pages xiv and xvi for a complete description of these strands.

Objects and Places   Form as Illusion and Reality

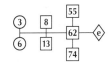

LESSON 7

Train Your Visual Memory

Suggested Art Materials

See the art materials list for this lesson in the student book.

Helpful Teaching Hints

- Arrange a still life of interesting objects on a tray. Place it near a bright light. Have students observe the objects for several minutes. Remove the arrangement and ask students to close their eyes to visualize the objects. Then have them make sketches of the arrangement from memory. When their sketches are finished, compare them to the actual still life arrangement*.
- Review the various shading techniques on page 219 of the student text and encourage students to try a new one.

Additional Materials Needed:

*tray, flood lamp, still life objects

Book Strand

Book strand 7, Objects and Places, includes this lesson in its diagram, pictured below. See page xiv for a complete description of this strand.

Objects and Places

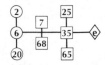

LESSON 8

A Three-Quarter View Portrait

Suggested Art Materials

See the art materials list for this lesson in the student book.

Planning Ahead

Collect reproductions of portraits, done in pencil, which show a three-quarter view of the subject. (Drawings by Michelangelo, Leonardo da Vinci, and Holbein should be useful here.)

Helpful Teaching Hints

- Have students look at the three-quarter view examples. They will want to notice different facial features, expressions, and unique characteristics.
- Mention to students that half of any person's face is usually different from the other half; one eyebrow may be higher or thicker than the other, one nostril larger or smaller, and so on. Have them look for these details in their model before starting to draw.
- When students are sketching the eyes, nose, mouth, and ears, point out that these features are

drawn best by using mere suggestions of lines and shapes and by shading. Refer to Picasso's drawing on page 20 of the student text as an excellent example.
- Suggest to the students that they seat their selected model near a strong light source to increase the contrast of lights and darks on the facial features.
- Stress that sketching the head shape and facial features very lightly in the beginning will make it easier to make adjustments and reduce the amount of erasing.

Book Strand

Book strand 12, Studying People, includes this lesson in its diagram, pictured below. See page xv for a complete description of this strand.

Studying People

LESSON 9

Old and Young People

Suggested Art Materials

See the art materials list for this lesson in the student book.

Planning Ahead

Collect photographs and drawings of young and old people. Also collect visuals of Native Americans, Eskimos, and members of other ethnic groups. Discuss how the features of people vary, and how the lives of older people are reflected in their faces.

Helpful Teaching Hints

- Have a young child or an older person model for the class.
- Have students create a photomontage consisting of faces cut from magazines.*

Additional Materials Needed:
*magazines, glue, scissors, cardboard

Book Strand

Book strand 5, Contrast and Opposites, and book strand 12, Studying People, include this lesson in their diagrams, pictured below. See pages xiv and xv, respectively, for complete descriptions of these strands.

Contrast and Opposites   Studying People

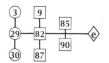   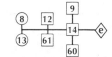

LESSON 10

Sketching in the Style of Leonardo da Vinci

Suggested Art Materials

See the art materials list in the student book.

Planning Ahead

Be prepared to show reproductions of works by Leonardo da Vinci, or a film or slide show of his work. Discuss the role and importance of creative people in society.

Helpful Teaching Hints

- Have each student tell about his or her choice of subject and what medium will be used to render it.
- Demonstrate how to use a variety of media to achieve different effects of light and dark.

Book Strand

Book strand 11, Learning from Artists, includes this lesson in its diagram, pictured below. See page xv for a complete description of this strand.

Learning from Artists

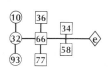

LESSON 11

Exaggerated Drawings and Caricatures

Suggested Art Materials

See the art materials list in the student book.

Planning Ahead

- Alert students ahead of time to start looking for political cartoons and caricatures in newspapers and magazines.

- Be prepared to discuss the role of political cartoons and satire in our culture.

Helpful Teaching Hints

Show a variety of current and historical political cartoons to point out that this is a valid art form with a long past.
Additional Materials Needed:
examples of works by Thomas Nast, Gustave Doré, and Daumier

Related Art Career (cartoonist)

Cartooning is a specialized career based on the same education as that of illustrator. (See Lesson 35.) The cartoonist strives to develop a unique style that, when combined with the written word, will convey a message or make a point. Some cartoonists prefer to concentrate their art in specialized areas, such as witty humor, political satire, or adventure. In addition to creating cartoon art for the printed medium, the world of animation beckons some cartoonists to apply their art to television, videos, or movies.

Have students create a list of their favorite cartoon characters from comic strips, comic books, television and movies. Discuss with them how individual artists' styles have contributed to the creation of unique characters with definite personality traits. Discuss the differences between the skills and techniques required to create animated cartoons and printed comics.

Book Strand

Book strand 9, Artistic Messages, and book strand 13, Fantasy and Distortion, include this lesson in their diagrams, pictured below. See pages xiv and xv, respectively, for complete descriptions of these strands.

Artistic Messages   Fantasy and Distortion

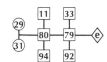   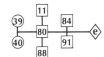

LESSON 12

Portrait of Hands

Suggested Art Materials

See the art materials list for this lesson in the student book.

Helpful Teaching Hints

- Display drawings by well-known artists that particularly emphasize the hands.*
- Invite a mime or ballet dancer to demonstrate for your class hand gestures and their importance in these arts.

Additional Materials Needed:
*reproductions of drawings by Dürer, Michelangelo, Leonardo da Vinci, Rembrandt, and Raphael

Book Strand

Book strand 12, Studying People, includes this lesson in the diagram, pictured below. See page xv for a complete description of this strand.

Studying People

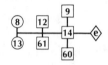

LESSON 13

Human Measurements

Suggested Art Materials

See the art materials list for this lesson in the student book.

Helpful Teaching Hints

- Using a tape measure, compare the body proportions of a tall and a short student to see how height affects the relationship of basic body parts.
- Have students select a part of the body (head, hand, or foot) to use as a basis for measurement. Each student will then use the length of that part as a measure of other body parts to note relationships and proportions. Then have students compare these measurements for sections of the body, such as shoulder to waist, neck to heel, shoulder to fingertips, hip to knee, knee to ankle, and so on. Unique body characteristics, for example, short-waisted or long-waisted forms, may become apparent in this activity, while reinforcing common body proportions, regardless of height.
- As students are experimenting with different poses, mention that those which *do not* require foreshortening will be easier for them to draw. Foreshortening is one of the most difficult aspects of drawing realistic figures and is usually reserved for advanced classes. Less experienced students will

probably experience frustration if they attempt a pose which requires it. To demonstrate foreshortening, ask a student to pose with any portion of a leg or arm extended straight toward the other students.

Additional Materials Needed:
large sheets of butcher paper, tape measure

Book Strand

Book strand 12, Studying People, and book strand 17, Relationships in Design, include this lesson in their diagrams, pictured below. See page xv and xvi for a complete description of these strands.

Studying People   Relationships in Design

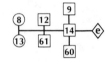   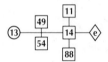

LESSON 14

People in Action

Suggested Art Materials

See the art materials list in the student book.

Planning Ahead

Prepare photographs of people in action, using sheets of clear plastic or acetate as overlays. Display these, using an overhead projector and showing with a ruler and a grease pencil that the bodily proportions are the same for figures in action as for figures in repose, even though movement can appear to change them.

Additional Materials Needed:
photographs of people in action, acetate, overhead projector, grease pencil

Helpful Teaching Hints

- Arrange for the students to make sketches of people involved in athletic events or gym classes.
- Ask an athlete to model action poses for your class.
- Point out to students that gesture drawing is a very free, loose technique in contrast to the previous lesson which called for concentration on specific proportions.
- Have students "loosen up" for the gesture drawing of several quick poses by sketching in the air with their finger while looking at the model.
- As students are adding details to their finished

piece, mention that less is often better in artwork. A few shaded areas will create more emphasis than shading throughout the entire piece.

Book Strand

Book strand 12, Studying People, includes this lesson in its diagram, pictured below. See page xv for a complete description of this strand.

Studying People

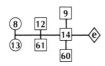

LESSON 15

Geometric Shapes

Suggested Art Materials

See the art materials list for this lesson in the student book.

Planning Ahead

To help students think geometrically, outline with colored tape geometric shapes in the classroom, or cover them with colored paper.
Additional Materials Needed:
colored tape, colored paper

Helpful Teaching Hints

• Try to procure a drawing board for each student.
• Collect reproductions of works by artists who use geometric shapes. These could include current graphic works used in advertising. Show how the use of geometric shapes in artworks reflects a man-made environment.*
Additional Materials Needed:
*reproductions of works by Picasso, Cézanne, Leger, the Cubists, and modern graphic artists

Book Strand

Book strand 2, Creating with Lines, and book strand 15, Learning About Shape, include this lesson in their diagrams, pictured below. See pages xiii and xv for a complete description of these strands.

Creating with Lines   Learning About Shape

   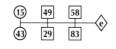

LESSON 16

Showing Depth and Distance

Suggested Art Materials

See the art materials list in the student book.

Planning Ahead

Prepare photographs of cityscapes so that they have overlays of clear plastic or acetate attached.
Additional Materials Needed:
photographs of cityscapes, acetate

Helpful Teaching Hints

• Display your prepared photographs, using the overhead projector. Ask volunteers to find and draw in the horizon line, vanishing point, and chief horizontal and vertical lines of each picture.*
• Where possible, take the students outside and have them locate the horizon line and vanishing point.
• The students would enjoy using photographs that portray local streets or scenes they are familiar with.**
Additional Materials Needed:
*overhead projector, grease pencils
**photographs of local scenes

Safety Precautions

Use glue only in a well-ventilated area.

Book Strand

Book strand 6, Near and Far, includes this lesson in its diagram, pictured below. See page xiv for a complete description of this strand.

Near and Far

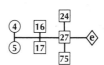

LESSON 17

Bird's-Eye View

Suggested Art Materials

See the art materials list in the student book.

Helpful Teaching Hints

On the floor, build a model city using toy cars, children's blocks, etc. Have your students draw the city as seen from a standing position.

Additional Materials Needed:
building blocks, toys, miniature buildings, etc.

Book Strand

Book strand 6, Near and Far, and book strand 10, Visions and Feelings, include this lesson in their diagrams, pictured below. See pages xiv and xv, respectively, for complete descriptions of these strands.

Near and Far   Visions and Feelings

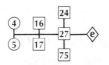 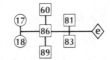

LESSON 18

Unusual Angles

Suggested Art Materials

See the art materials list in the student book.

Helpful Teaching Hints

• Ask the students if they have ever viewed themselves in distorted mirrors, such as are found in fun houses. If so, they can use their visual memories to draw a picture of how they looked.
• Have the students view the world through curved glass or magnifying glasses and draw what they see.*

Additional Materials Needed:
*curved glass, magnifying glasses

Book Strand

Book strand 10, Visions and Feelings, includes this lesson in its diagram, pictured below. See page xv for a complete description of this strand.

Visions and Feelings

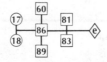

LESSON 19

Different Styles of Drawing

Suggested Art Materials

See the art materials list in the student book.

Helpful Teaching Hints

• Display various reproductions, and have the students guess what medium was used for each, according to the effects achieved. (Many libraries carry fine print catalogs which contain clear reproductions.)
• Demonstrate, or have volunteers demonstrate, how to properly use the various media.

Book Strand

Book strand 14, The Road to Abstraction, includes this lesson in its diagram, pictured below. See page xv for a complete description of this strand.

The Road to Abstraction

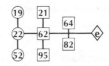

LESSON 20

Drawing Animals

Suggested Art Materials

See the art materials list in the student book.

Helpful Teaching Hints

• Arrange for the class to visit a zoo, a farm, a ranch, or a pet store, where they can freely make sketches of the animals.
• Organize a pet show, where the students can bring their pets to display while also having an opportunity to sketch animals in action.

Book Strand

Book strand 7, Objects and Places, includes this lesson in its diagram, pictured below. See page xiv for a complete description of this strand.

Objects and Places

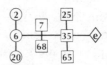

EXPLORING ART

Sketchbook Animals

See pages 2 and 3 for an explanation and teaching suggestions.

Unit II
Color and Composition

Learning Objectives

In this unit, the students will achieve the following objectives:

Understanding Art

- Understand vocabulary terms related to color
- Understand that different paints and painting techniques create different effects
- Identify and apply principles of composition, using color and line

Creating Art

- Learn to mix colors, tints, and shades
- Learn to apply color, using a variety of media and painting techniques
- Learn to handle and use art tools correctly, including various types of brushes
- Learn to show linear and atmospheric perspective in painting
- Learn to mat and mount finished artwork

Appreciating Art

- Understand the historic and cultural importance of Renaissance, Oriental, and Mexican art
- Explore innovative painting styles of well-known American artists
- Appreciate the differing innovative styles of three Postimpressionists

Unit Strands

A strand consists of a group of related lessons where the student is expected to begin with one of the lesson choices available on the far left (arranged vertically), complete it, proceed horizontally to the next group of choices, make a choice and complete the lesson, and so forth, until the entire sequence has been completed. (See page v for complete instructions on using strands.) The unit strands for this unit are diagramed below and at the top of the next column.

Strand D: Exploring Color

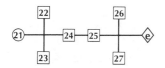

Strand E: Painting Styles and Techniques

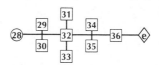

Background Information

Unit II builds on the basic skills students developed in the drawing lessons. It introduces advanced concepts of composition, color manipulation using more sophisticated painting techniques, creative exploration of different styles of painting, and painting concepts of past and current cultures.

Lesson 21, A Study in Color, and Lesson 22, Colors, Tints, and Shades, introduce basic color concepts, defining the terms *primary, complementary, value, tint, shade, intensity,* and *contrasting.* Students are asked to show their understanding of color concepts through a variety of preliminary exercises. They then use their knowledge of value, tint, and shade to compose a monochrome painting in Lesson 23 and a painting showing atmospheric perspective in Lesson 24.

Lesson 25, A Tempera Batik Landscape, offers students a chance to experiment with a batik-like technique in producing a stylized landscape picture. Attention is called for in planning and executing the design, because beyond a certain point in the process, the technique does not allow for changes or repainting.

Lesson 26, Using Watercolor Paints, Lesson 27, Painting from Back to Front, and Lesson 28, Dry Brush Painting, introduce the basics of watercolor painting. Techniques of preparing the paper for painting, laying on a wash, and handling paint using wet and dry brush techniques are covered. Emphasis is on the thought and pre-planning necessary to achieve white highlights with a transparent paint. Opaque colors are used afterwards to create dark values. Lesson 27 also calls on the skills learned in the earlier lesson on atmospheric perspective, while Lesson 28 requires that the brush be used in both a drawing and painting manner, to create textural effects.

Lesson 29, Shadows and Silhouettes, and Lesson 30, Showing Reflections, pose two different painting problems relating to use of light in a composition. Lesson 29 emphasizes the effect of a bright, single light source and the creation of strong light and dark values. Lesson 30 requires students to observe and replicate the effect of diffused light on a landscape reflected in water. Students must show balance, contrast, pattern, rhythm, and unity in their compositions.

Lesson 31 introduces some of the philosophical concepts which influence Oriental art and asks students to study the style and techniques used in Oriental painting. The typical bamboo brush, India ink, and soft-toned watercolor washes are essential tools and techniques in this lesson.

Lesson 32, The Renaissance, presents introductory material on the importance of this period in the history of Western art. Students are asked to draw a draped garment, much in the same way apprentices were required to do long ago. This exercise calls for careful observation and attention to details.

Lesson 33, Great Mexican Artists, increases student awareness of the art concepts and forms that emerged at the time of the 1910 Mexican Revolution. To promote the understanding of another culture's art, students are asked to think and paint in the manner of the outstanding Mexican muralists. Students are encouraged to portray current social and/or political themes in a mural of their own.

Lesson 34, American Painters, focuses on the innovative styles of Edward Hopper, Stuart Davis, and Georgia O'Keeffe. This lesson helps to widen students' knowledge of American painters and explains their work in the context of American art history. It also encourages students to analyze their own emerging styles and to try out different approaches to painting. Lesson 35, Picturing a Part of America, continues the exploration of the differing painting styles of American painters, this time in the landscape genre. Students compose and paint scenes of their own choice, utilizing painting skills and techniques learned throughout this unit.

Lesson 36, The Fathers of Modern Art, concentrates on three Postimpressionist painters—Van Gogh, Gauguin, and Cézanne. It discusses their compositional concepts and highly individualistic painting styles. Each student is asked to compose a picture and paint it in the style of one of these masters.

Strategies for Motivation

This painting unit builds on the foundational skills and artistic concepts developed in the drawing unit. It continues to expand the learner's capabilities by introducing more sophisticated approaches to design and composition and more demanding watercolor and brush techniques. Students are encouraged to analyze their own and others' painting styles and to make significant choices concerning their own development as artists. Students will be more motivated to engage fully in these activities if they feel prepared to discuss artworks intelligently. Encouraging the students to take their own efforts seriously will also help. Following are some suggestions for developing these two attitudes.

- Invite a local watercolor artist to class to talk about and demonstrate watercolor techniques.
- Show slides/films that demonstrate particular techniques.
- Show slides/films of artists featured in this unit.
- Work with students to arrange outdoor painting sessions.
- Invite Oriental and Mexican-American artists to talk about and demonstrate their art.
- Insist on students keeping sketchbooks to be turned in periodically for evaluation.
- Make matting and mounting of final projects a standard requirement, and require students to keep portfolios. These activities will help students develop professional attitudes about their work.
- Have an end-of-semester public exhibit of students' work, so the students may share and discuss their work with guests.

Extending Art

Exploring Art

In this Exploring Art feature, students combine art skills with English composition skills by writing a short paper about the style of a favorite master artist. Remind students that the paper should include three elements: a brief biography of the artist, a detailed analysis of the artist's style and techniques (taking into account the effects of major events in the artist's life), and a discussion of how one specific work by the artist exemplifies his or her style. Refer students to their English texts for techniques of expository writing. To further extend this lesson:

- Help students to see that parallel trends often occur in art and music. Prepare a slide display of artworks from a particular period, and accompany it with music from the same period. For example, music by Debussy and Ravel could accompany work by Impressionists, while music by Mozart and Vivaldi could accompany works by Neoclassicists. Discuss similarities in the musicians' and artists' styles. Then invite students to find contemporary artworks that show stylistic features also evident in contemporary music.

- Assign students to research famous art forgeries and the methods used to uncover them. First, arrange for the librarian to familiarize students with research techniques. Then instruct students to use the *Reader's Guide* and card catalog to find information and prepare short research reports. These reports can be presented to the class.

Additional Activities

Lessons in this unit may be expanded in a number of ways:

- Have the students paint a series of paintings based on their neighborhoods—at different seasons, in different lights, perhaps even in different decades.
- Ask students to make many small, quick painting sketches and mount them beside the final paintings to show how their work evolved/changed.
- Appoint a committee of students to keep track of museum or gallery exhibits relevant to class work.

Evaluating Procedures

As noted in the introduction to this book, evaluation in art classes poses unique problems for the teacher. (See pages vii and viii) The *Learning Outcomes* address the need for self-evaluation and test the students on the details of what they have learned. However, the teacher still needs some means of determining the extent of a student's application of specifics to a solid core of basic art knowledge. Three things are involved in this type of evaluation:

1. A written test of the student's recall of important facts
2. An examination of the student's artwork in terms of the achievement of certain previously stated goals
3. An oral discussion with the student, involving his or her comments on a particular piece of art

Explanations of these three evaluative components for Unit II follow.

Vocabulary

Students who complete this unit should be able to define and correctly use the art terms listed below. A written test on the unit should, then, be based on these terms.

abstract	overlapping
architecture	path of vision
atmospheric	pattern
perspective	Postimpressionist
background	primary color
balance	Renaissance
cast shadows	rhythm
center of interest	secondary color
complementary color	shade
contrast	silhouette
distortion	still life
emphasis	style
foreground	tempera
hard-edge painting	tempera batik
horizon line	theme
hues	tint
Impressionist	tone
intensity	transparent
landscape	two-dimensional
linear perspective	unity
media	value
monochrome	wash
mural	watercolor
opaque	

Skills

The artworks students create in this unit should meet the standards listed below. Be certain that the students are aware of these standards both as they plan and as they work. You may choose to keep this list posted throughout the time spent on this unit.

- Brushes and media are used in a variety of ways for a variety of effects.
- Colors are mixed and used effectively to complement the mood of the painting.
- Atmospheric and linear perspective, overlapping, detail, and size are used appropriately to indicate distance.
- The effects of light are noticed and portrayed.

Application of Knowledge

Listening to a student talk about an artwork can give you a true sense of how much the student understands the basic elements and principles of design. However, the planning behind such a discussion is important. First, the work to be discussed must be chosen in advance by the teacher. Questions must be written that will lead the student into the correct areas of emphasis. Last, the discussion should be arranged to take place on a one-to-one basis, so that the more reticent students are not left out of a group discussion.

A suggested artwork to use for discussion purposes in this unit is the painting by Robert Wood entitled *Autumn Glade.*

Supplementary Materials and Resources

Teacher Resources

Bartlett, Adam. *Drawing and Painting the Landscape.* Secaucus, New Jersey: Chartwell Books, Inc., 1982.

This comprehensive book includes techniques for drawing with pencil and with pen and ink, and how-to instructions for using pastels, watercolors, gouache, tempera, oils, and acrylics. A glossary of terms is included. Excellent black-and-white and color photographs supplement the text.

Chase, Alice Elizabeth. *Famous Artists of the Past.* New York: Platt and Munk, 1964.

This book includes 27 artists from Michelangelo and Leonardo da Vinci to French Impressionists. It contains 177 reproductions, 44 of which are in acceptable color. Text about each artist includes comments on artistic achievement as well as biographical information. (This book is suitable for students also.)

Goodrich, Lloyd. *Three Centuries of American Art.* New York: Fredrick A. Prager, 1966.

A pictorial survey of work by leading artists from the past and present, this book gives about equal weight to 20th-century art and the past. The well-written text is supplemented by excellent color reproductions.

Simon, Matila. *The Shorewood Art Reference Guide,* Revised, 3rd ed. New York: Shorewood Reproductions, Inc., 1970.

This is a catalog of black-and-white photos of prints available from Shorewood, accompanied by brief descriptions, with a longer essay about each artist. Included are artists from the Italian Renaissance to 20th-century American art. Oriental and Mexican art are also represented. The book includes series on the use of color, use of line, shape, balance, composition, etc.

Slide Buyer's Guide, 4th edition, published by the Mid-America College Art Association Visual Resources Committee. Printed by the University of Missouri, Kansas City: 1980.

This is a comprehensive listing of slide sources. Copies are available from: Arlene Zelda Richardson, Slide Library, Room 2010, Fine Arts Center, University of New Mexico, Albuquerque, New Mexico 87131.

Student Resources

Raboff, Ernest. *van Gogh.* Garden City, New York: Doubleday and Co., 1978.

Books in this series include those on Klee, Chagall, Renoir, Picasso, and Leonardo da Vinci. Short and colorful, they include reproductions of the artists' works and analyses by the authors.

Weiss, Harvey. *Paint, Brush and Pallette.* New York: Young Scott Books, 1966.

This book covers color, color mixing, shapes and forms, light and shadow, and use of materials. It also includes a how-to section on figures, landscapes, oils and watercolors, and pastels. Included are reproductions of works by van Gogh, Miro, Degas, Renoir, Monet, Rembrandt and others.

TEACHING SUGGESTIONS for Lessons 21–36

LESSON 21

A Study in Color

Suggested Art Materials

See the art materials list for this lesson in the student book.

Planning Ahead

Go over primary, secondary, and complementary colors with students, using the color chart on page 3.
Additional Materials Needed:
color wheel or chart

Helpful Teaching Hints

- Hang prisms in sunlight so the students can see the effects of colors.*
- Collect sample paint chips from a paint or hardware store, and cut them up. Have the students create mosaic pictures using primary and complementary colors.**

Additional Materials Needed:
 * prisms
**paint color samples

Book Strand

Book strand 14, The Road to Abstraction, includes this lesson in its diagram, pictured below. See page xv for a complete description of this strand.

The Road to Abstraction

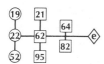

LESSON 22

Colors, Tints, and Shades

Suggested Art Materials

See the art materials list in the student book.

Planning Ahead

Prepare a color chart which explains visually the terms *hue, value, intensity, tint,* and *shade.*

Helpful Teaching Hints

Have the students mark off the sections of their designs with masking tape if they have trouble making hard-line edges.
Additional Materials Needed:
masking tape

Book Strand

Book strand 14, The Road to Abstraction, includes this lesson in its diagram, pictured below. See page xv for a complete description of this strand.

The Road to Abstraction

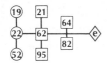

LESSON 23

A Monochrome Painting

Suggested Art Materials

See the art materials list in the student book.

Planning Ahead

Collect monochromatic paintings by well-known artists (Picasso, Cassatt, Raphael, Degas) to show as examples.

Helpful Teaching Hints

Have the students look through tinted glass or dark glasses at a still life set-up. This will help them understand the idea of painting in a single hue.
Additional Materials Needed:
tinted glass or dark glasses

Book Strand

Book strand 1, Exploring with Paint, includes this lesson in its diagram, pictured below. See page xiii for a complete description of this strand.

Exploring with Paint

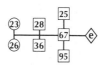

LESSON 24

Showing Distance with Color

Suggested Art Materials

See the art materials list for this lesson in the student book.

Planning Ahead

Collect reproductions of works showing atmospheric perspective. (Japanese prints are good examples.)

Helpful Teaching Hints

Teach the students how to correctly mat and mount their works after one of these early lessons, so they can begin to view their work more professionally.
Additional Materials Needed:
mat board, mat knives

Safety Precautions

Teach the students to use mat knives properly (to cut away from the body and to keep fingers out of the cutting path) and to store them safely.

Book Strand

Book strand 6, Near and Far, includes this lesson in its diagram, pictured at the top of the next page. See page xiv for a complete description of this strand.

Near and Far

LESSON 25

A Tempera Batik Landscape

Suggested Art Materials

See the art materials list for this lesson in the student book.

Planning Ahead

Collect pieces of batik or batik-like fabric to show the students.

Helpful Teaching Hints

- Encourage the students to keep their designs simple.
- Supply rubber gloves for the students to wear during the rinsing stage.*

Additional Materials Needed:
* rubber gloves

Safety Precautions

India ink is permanent and easily absorbed into the skin. Have the students wear paint shirts and use newspapers to protect work surfaces. Urge them to wash skin immediately if ink is contacted.

Book Strands

Book strand 1, Exploring with Paint, and book strand 7, Objects and Places, include this lesson in their diagrams, pictured below. See pages xiii and xiv, respectively, for complete descriptions of these strands.

Exploring with Paint   Objects and Places

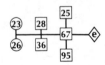 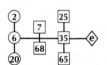

LESSON 26

Using Watercolor Paints

Suggested Art Materials

See the art materials list for this lesson in the student book.

Planning Ahead

Invite a watercolor artist to demonstrate technique for the students, or show a film of an artist working in watercolors.

Helpful Teaching Hints

Demonstrate how to wet and tape watercolor paper to a drawing board. If possible, have a variety of papers for the students to experiment with as they use different wash and dry-brush techniques.
Additional Materials Needed:
masking tape; drawing boards; different weights, types of watercolor paper

Book Strand

Book strand 1, Exploring with Paint, includes this lesson in its diagram, pictured below. See page xiii for a complete description of this strand.

Exploring with Paint

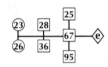

LESSON 27

Painting from Back to Front

Suggested Art Materials

See the art materials list for this lesson in the student book.

Planning Ahead

Here again, a demonstration by a local watercolor artist or the instructor would be helpful. Techniques taught in several of these lessons could be shown in one demonstration.

Helpful Teaching Hints

- Taping paper to drawing boards is helpful to prevent puddling. An alternative is to have the students initially do several washes. As these dry partially, they can be used.
- Inexpensive drawing boards may be made by cutting masonite or light-weight plywood into small sections.

Book Strand

Book strand 6, Near and Far, includes this lesson in its diagram, pictured at the top of the next page. See page xiv for a complete description of this strand.

Near and Far

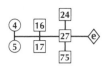

LESSON 28

Dry Brush Painting

Suggested Art Materials

See the art materials list in the student book.

Planning Ahead

Collect and exhibit examples of watercolors that exemplify this technique—Dürer's *Piece of Lawn*, for instance.

Helpful Teaching Hints

Point out to the students that with the dry-brush technique they are drawing with the brush, as well as painting. They are, in fact, combining the two skills.

Book Strand

Book strand 1, Exploring with Paint, includes this lesson in its diagram, pictured below. See page xiii for a complete description of this strand.

Exploring with Paint

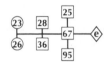

LESSON 29

Shadows and Silhouettes

Suggested Art Materials

See the art materials list in the student book.

Planning Ahead

Reproductions of works by Georges de La Tour, French School (1593–1652), would help to dramatize this lesson. La Tour is noted for unusual lighting effects in his paintings.

Helpful Teaching Hints

Set up a scene in the classroom, using real models. Use floodlights to create a strong backlight.
Additional Materials Needed:
portable floodlights

Book Strands

Book strand 5, Contrast and Opposites, and book strand 9, Artistic Messages, include this lesson in their diagrams, pictured below. See page xiv for complete descriptions of these strands.

LESSON 30

Showing Reflections

Suggested Art Materials

See the art materials list for this lesson in the student book.

Planning Ahead

Collect reproductions of works by Canaletto, Manet, Turner, and others who are known for painting water scenes.

Helpful Teaching Hints

If possible, arrange a field trip to a nearby pond, stream, lake, swimming pool, or ocean. It is always preferable to paint from the real thing.

Book Strand

Book strand 5, Contrast and Opposites, and book strand 20, Rhythmic Repetition, include this lesson in their diagrams, pictured below. See pages xiv and xvi for a complete description of these strands.

LESSON 31

Oriental Art Styles

Suggested Art Materials

See the art materials list for this lesson in the student book.

Planning Ahead

This lesson affords an excellent opportunity to invite an Oriental artist to demonstrate. As an alternative to a live demonstration, try to procure a film showing Oriental brush techniques, or collect reproductions of Oriental work and discuss how the particular effects are created.

Helpful Teaching Hints

Procure Oriental brushes so the students can work with the real thing.
Additional Materials Needed:
Oriental brushes

Safety Precautions

Both permanent and non-waterproof inks stain badly. If ink gets on skin, wash it off immediately.

Book Strand

Book strand 9, Artistic Messages, and book strand 18, Famous Styles and Artists, include this lesson in their diagrams, pictured below. See pages xiv and xvi for a complete description of these strands.

Artistic Messages   Famous Styles and Artists

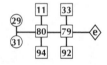 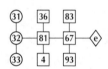

da Vinci, Michelangelo, Raphael, and others to show that master artists sketch, copy, and refine their art. This will help the students understand that artists of this period were primarily concerned with realistic portrayals of all subject matter.

- Encourage students to bring in fabric pieces of different textures, such as satin, velour, corduroy, velveteen, or silk. Have students observe the effects of light on these various textures.
- Discuss the different kinds of shading techniques that might be used to depict the various fabric textures.
- Remind students to consider the principles of art as they plan how the fabric will be draped over the chair.
- Have students discuss how the addition of tempera paint changes the look of the draped fabric.

Book Strand

Book strand 11, Learning from Artists, includes this lesson in its diagram, pictured below. See page xv for a complete description of this strand.

Learning from Artists

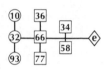

LESSON 32

The Renaissance

Suggested Art Materials

See the art materials list for this lesson in the student book.

Planning Ahead

Begin by explaining the importance of the Renaissance to Western culture. (It ushered in the birth of cities as we know them; the exploration of the New World occurred; and works of art, literature, and music which we still enjoy today were created.) Try to give the students a holistic view of the Renaissance by reading aloud some of the poetry of the period and by showing reproductions of views of cities, gardens, or architecture. Play some recorded music of the period.

Helpful Teaching Hints

- Show examples from the sketchbooks of Leonardo

LESSON 33

Great Mexican Artists

Suggested Art Materials

See the art materials list in the student book.

Planning Ahead

This lesson offers an opportunity to show how artists participate in the social and political events of their countries. Mexican history, poetry, and music could be incorporated.

Helpful Teaching Hints

- Review with the students the events of the 1910 Mexican Revolution.
- Encourage the students to read newspapers or watch TV news for several days, noting down which issues interest them most. They can choose mural themes from their notes.
- Have the students decide where their pictures or murals will be displayed before beginning the

designs. Designs should be appropriate to the places of display and to intended audiences.

Book Strand

Book strand 9, Artistic Messages, and book strand 10, Famous Styles and Artists, include this lesson in their diagrams, pictured below. See pages xiv and xv for a complete description of these strands.

Artistic Messages   Famous Styles and Artists

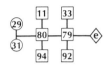 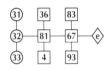

LESSON 34

American Painters

Suggested Art Materials

See the art materials list for this lesson in the student book.

Planning Ahead

This lesson could be expanded by showing examples of other American artists, including Grant Wood, Grandma Moses, and Robert Rauschenberg, all of whom had/have distinctive styles.
Additional Materials Needed:
reproductions of works by as wide a selection as possible of past and present American artists

Helpful Teaching Hints

- Take the students to a retrospective show of an American artist. Discuss changes in style, growth.
- Ask an artist to talk about how his/her style has evolved, and why this is important to an artist.
- Mount an exhibit of students' work, and discuss how each student's has changed. Are visible styles emerging?

Related Art Career (fine artist)

The story of the starving artist is not a myth. Many who have chosen fine art painting as their career discover they can't count on earning a living from the sale of their work alone. Most turn to teaching or to other related applied arts jobs as secondary sources of income.

Attending a good art school is a beginning for those who wish to pursue a career in fine arts. However, artists must usually practice their craft for many years before they are able to develop a personal art style that will enhance their work and win them recognition in this highly competitive field. Most fine artists begin by displaying their work in local or regional art shows, exhibitions, or galleries on commission.

Contact a local art organization or gallery to find out when the work of local or regional artists may be on display and, if possible, take your students to see the exhibit.

Individual students may want to research the career of a well-known artist and present a report to the class.

Book Strand

Book strand 11, Learning from Artists, includes this lesson in its diagram, pictured below. See page xv for a complete description of this strand.

Learning from Artists

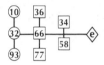

LESSON 35

Picturing a Part of America

Suggested Art Materials

See the art materials list for this lesson in the student book.

Planning Ahead

Give a slide show of past and/or current American landscape painters, to show how ways of depicting the landscape have changed. As an alternative, exhibit reproductions of paintings.

Helpful Teaching Hints

Have the students paint some of the local scenery, and ask them to look for fresh ways to see the familiar.

Related Art Career (book illustrator)

The book illustrator creates art to enhance or explain the printed page. This career in applied arts is one of the closest to fine arts. Illustrators often attend art school or college, working in a variety of media. Knowledge of printmaking, photography, and the mechanics of printing are also important. Technical courses in mechanical drafting are needed for some illustrators. Although a college degree is helpful, the quality and style of work in a strong portfolio is equally important. Successful illustrators become observers, readers, and researchers of the subject matter they are illustrating. In order to develop experience, contacts, and business knowledge, many illustrators begin their careers by working for an art service or group of illustrators who contract work with larger companies. Most illustrators prefer to work on a free-lance basis.

Have each student bring in a favorite illustrated book, short story, or article. As a group, discuss the various art styles and media used in the illustrated works. Have each student illustrate a cover for their favorite piece of non-illustrated prose or poetry. If possible, invite a book illustrator to class to discuss his or her artwork.

Book Strand

Book strand 7, Objects and Places, and book strand 19, Movement in Art, include this lesson in their diagrams, pictured below. See pages xiv and xvi for a complete description of these strands.

Objects and Places   Movement in Art

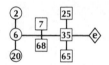 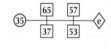

LESSON 36

The Fathers of Modern Art

Suggested Art Materials

See the art materials list in the student book.

Planning Ahead

Collect reproductions or slides that portray the colors and brushwork used by Van Gogh, Gauguin, and Cézanne.

Helpful Teaching Hints

• Set up a still life similar to one of Cézanne's, and have the students paint it.
• Ask the students to paint pictures of their bedrooms in the manner of Van Gogh (see The Artist's Room in Arles).

Book Strands

Book strand 1, Exploring with Paint, and book strand 11, Learning from Artists, include this lesson in their diagrams, pictured below. See pages xiii and xv, respectively, for complete descriptions of these strands.

Exploring with Paint   Learning from Artists

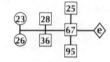 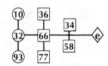

Exploring Art

Discovering a Painter's Style

See page 00 for an explanation and teaching suggestions.

Unit III
Design, Media, and Technique

Learning Objectives

In this unit, the students will achieve the following objectives:

Understanding Art

- Understand and correctly use vocabulary words related to color
- Understand realistic and abstract art and recognize their differences
- Relate art styles to the meanings behind them

Creating Art

- Learn and use the basic techniques of fabric art, including stitchery, weaving, appliqué, and macramé
- Distort images to produce certain effects
- Create basic print designs
- Employ correct proportions in letters used for graphic design
- Create unified compositions out of a variety of media

Appreciating Art

- Appreciate the role of decision-making skills in the creation of all art forms
- Notice and enjoy art in the environment
- Validate graphic arts, fabric arts, and block printing as legitimate art forms with recognized standards of excellence

Unit Strands

A strand consists of a group of related lessons where the student is expected to begin with one of the lesson choices available on the far left (arranged vertically), complete it, proceed horizontally to the next group of choices, make a choice and complete the lesson, and so forth, until the entire sequence has been completed. (See page v for complete instructions on using strands.) The unit strands for this unit are diagrammed at the top of the next column.

Strand F: Designing with Different Media

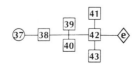

Strand G: Communicating Through Design

Background Information

In this unit, students explore a variety of graphic arts and crafts experiences, including lettering, poster design, block printing, and fabric arts. Emphasis is on creating designs of artistic merit and quality craftsmanship, using inexpensive or found materials.

The first two lessons in the unit stress simplicity, directness, and unity of design, as the students create collages out of paper and other suitable materials. The results are colorful and abstract designs. The term *abstract* takes on new meaning, however, in Lesson 39, Drawing Distortions, and Lesson 40, Slice, Twist, and Stretch. In these lessons the students create distorted *abstract* images, using either grids or photographs.

Lessons 41–45 are centered on the fabric arts. In the first three lessons of the series, the emphasis is on learning how to use a needle and yarn to create simple designs on fabric. Basic embroidery and appliqué techniques are introduced. Off-loom weaving is the focus of the next two lessons, in which the students are called upon to use their imaginations and manual dexterity to create woven sculptures and macramé.

The emphasis on creativity is continued in Lesson 46, Creativity with Beads. Students are given freedom in choosing found objects to use and in deciding what type of piece to create.

Lesson 47, Printmaking with Linoleum Blocks, introduces a basic printmaking technique. Students are required to create a design suitable for printing, transfer the design to a linoleum block, cut the design, and print it on paper.

Lessons 48–50 serve similarly as simple introductory lessons to basic art forms. Lesson 48, Visual Word Messages, teaches students to relate styles of lettering to meaning. Lesson 49, Drawing Letter Shapes, is an introduction to the art of calligraphy. Finally, Lesson 50, Designing a Poster, asks students to combine several skills to produce a unified, eye-catching composition.

Strategies for Motivation

In order to justify the breadth of the artistic experiences that students have in this unit, you will want to validate each art form as important. One way to do this is to expand on each form, showing ample examples of each. Another method is to ask the students to produce pieces of art that are significant to them as individuals. Following are some suggestions for such products.

- Have the students design a large, Matisse-like mural of paper cutouts to display in the classroom or the school hall.
- Have each student design, using embroidery or appliqué, his or her own heraldic symbol.
- Encourage the students to make numerous small macramé items: headbands, belts, earrings, etc.
- Have a fashion show in which students model their own handmade accessories.
- Have the students work in groups to design advertising promotions for a new product.

Extending Art

Exploring Art

This Exploring Art feature allows students to combine art skills with critical thinking skills by creating posters to advertise favorite books, movies, records, or tapes. Each poster should feature an attention-getting slogan as well as a unified design. Begin by discussing with students such advertising techniques as bandwagon, glittering generality, plain-folks appeal, snob appeal, and transfer. Ask them to find examples of each in magazines or on television. Then discuss the ways that words, color, and design can all appeal to emotions. Direct the students to decide which audience their posters will appeal to and to take into account audience interests and needs before starting on posters. Suggestions for further extending the lesson include:

- Arrange a tour of a printing facility. Ask the tour leader to show students how posters and other kinds of advertisements are actually manufactured.
- National, state, and local groups sponsor annual poster contests. (The U.S. Forest Service and the Milk Marketing Board are two examples.) Encourage students to enter such contests,

reminding them to again take the intended audiences into account as they create designs.

Additional Activities

Lessons in this unit may be extended in a number of ways to enhance their teaching potential and to provide additional motivational stimuli to students. Following are some suggestions.

- Have the students design a collage based on a theme that concerns them.
- Have the students design a large fabric mural that depicts a place in the local community. They can use block print, embroidery, appliqué, or a combination of techniques.
- Create a "gallery of rogues," using the distorted photos made in this unit.
- Have the students create a crazy zoo of animals, using the photo distortion method.
- Visit a crafts fair which includes exhibits of handmade jewelry, quilts, etc.

Evaluating Procedures

As noted in the introduction to this book, evaluation in art classes poses unique problems for the teacher. (See pages vii and viii) The Learning Outcomes address the need for self-evaluation and test the students on the details of what they have learned. However, the teacher still needs some means of determining the extent of a student's application of specifics to a solid core of basic art knowledge. Three things are involved in this type of evaluation:

1. A written test of the student's recall of important facts
2. An examination of the student's artwork in terms of the achievement of certain previously stated goals
3. An oral discussion with the student involving his or her comments on a particular piece of art

These three evaluative components for Unit III are explained below.

Vocabulary

Students who complete this unit should be able to define and correctly use the art terms listed on the following page. A written test on the unit should, then, be based on these terms.

abstract	legible
appliqué	loom
brayer	macramé
calligraphy	medium

center of interest
chisel
collage
complementary color
composition
contour
cool color
cutout
distortion
embroidery
found object
geometric
graphic artist
grid
gouging

movement
nib
realistic
rhythm
stitchery
tapestry
tempera
theme
transfer
unity
warm color
warp
weft
woodcut
verbalize
visualize

Skills

The artworks students create in this unit should meet the standards listed below. Be certain that the students are aware of these standards both as they plan and as they work. You may choose to keep this list posted throughout the time spent on this unit.
Collage:
• Colors and shapes reflect the mood of the design.
• Unity and a center of interest are important features.
• There is variety in the colors, patterns, and textures used.
Stitchery and Textiles:
• Variety is achieved in the design by the juxtaposition of various stitches, colors, and/or textures.
Printmaking:
• Time is taken to cut the design clearly and correctly.
• The design prints right side up, revealing the student's understanding of the reverse nature of the printing process.
Graphics:
• The style of the letters and design reflects the meaning.
• The letters are proportional and legible.

Application of Knowledge

Listening to a student talk about an artwork can give you a true sense of how much the student understands the basic elements and principles of design. However, the planning behind such a discussion is important. First, the work to be discussed must be chosen in advance and studied by the teacher. Questions must be written that will lead the student into the correct areas of emphasis. Last,

the discussion should be arranged to take place on a one-to-one basis so that the more reticent students are not left out of a group discussion.

Suggested artworks to use for discussion purposes in this unit are any of the posters which are part of the series entitled *Los Angeles Bicentennial 1781–1981*. Each poster is by a different artist, and a wide variety of styles and media is represented.

Supplementary Materials and Resources

Teacher Resources

Chase, Patti with Mimi Dolbier. *The Contemporary Quilt, New American Quilts and Fabric Arts.* New York: E.P. Dutton, 1978.
This book includes color photos of quilts, wall hangings, appliquéd and quilted fabric pictures, clothing, and three-dimensional work.

Colby, Averil. *Patchwork*. London: B.T. Batsford, 1958.
This is a classic, first published in 1958 and now available in paperback. It describes the history of appliqué and patchwork quilting. Many how-to instructions, black-and-white photographs, and diagrams accompany the text.

Harvey, Virginia I. *Macramé, the Art of Creative Knotting*. New York: Van Nostrand Reinhold Co., 1967.
This book gives the historical background of macramé along with excellent instructions on how to create macramé projects. Included are clear black-and-white photographs and diagrams.

Learn How Book. No. 170-D. Stamford, CT: Coates and Clark, Inc., 1975.
This pamphlet, available in sewing and crafts stores, includes instructions on making basic embroidery stitches.

The New American Quilt. Asheville, NC: Lark Communications Corp., 1981.
This book is published in conjunction with "Quilt National," the only juried competition for contemporary quilters. Featured are photographs of original designs and a statement by each artist represented.

Seagroatt, Margaret. *A Basic Textile Book*. New York: Van Nostrand Reinhold Co., 1975.
Covered in this book are discussions of the natures of fibers, dyeing, spinning, and weaving techniques; helpful photographs and diagrams; and an excellent chapter on the educational value of creating textiles.

Weaving, Techniques and Projects. Menlo Park, CA: Lane Books, 1975.
This excellent, inexpensive paperback gives a brief history of weaving, covers terms and the theory of design, and introduces the techniques of weaving and dyeing. It is well-illustrated with photographs and diagrams.

Student Resources

Beaney, Jan. *The Young Embroiderer*. New York: Frederick Warne and Co., Inc., 1968.
This book covers decision-making concerning choice of materials, equipment, and basic stitches. It discusses how to develop designs, and gives directions for how-to projects. Black-and-white photographs of historic pieces of embroidery are included.

Lightbody, Donna M. *Let's Knot, A Macramé Book*. New York: Lothrop, Lee and Shepard Co., 1972.
This book gives a brief history of macramé and includes step-by-step directions for creating belts, necklaces, plant holders, bookmarks, and bags. Clear black-and-white photographs are included.

Parker, Xenia Ley. *A Beginner's Book of Off-loom Weaving*. New York: Dodd, Mead and Co., 1978.
Covered in this book are a variety of off-loom weaving techniques. Yarns, threads, fibers, coiling and weaving in the round, basket-making, and crochet are among the topics discussed. The directions are clear and easy to follow; they are accompanied by diagrams and photographs of examples.

Wilson, Erica. *Fun with Crewel Embroidery*. New York: Charles Scribner's Sons, 1965.
This is a good basic book for beginning embroiderers. Discussions of materials, tools and basic stitches are accompanied by black-and-white diagrams and photographs.

TEACHING SUGGESTIONS for Lessons 37–50

LESSON 37

Drawing with Scissors

Suggested Art Materials

See the art materials list for this lesson in the student book.

Planning Ahead

Show a slide show or film about Matisse's paper figures.

Helpful Teaching Hints

- Point out that sharply angled shapes complement bright colors well, while smoothly curving shapes complement pastels.
- Have the students name one another's works according to their initial reactions.
- Put all the designs together to create one big, colorful display.

Safety Precautions

Use glue only in a well-ventilated area.

Book Strand

Book strand 3, Designing with Shapes and Objects, includes this lesson in its diagram, pictured below. See page xiv for a complete description of this strand.

Designing with Shapes and Objects

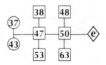

LESSON 38

Mixed Media Collage

Suggested Art Materials

See the art materials list for this lesson in the student book.

Planning Ahead

Collect, or have students collect, a large variety of materials suitable for collage work; have plenty to choose from.

Helpful Teaching Hints

Show reproductions of collages by Picasso or Leger, for inspiration.

Safety Precautions

Use glue only in a well-ventilated area. If India ink gets on your skin, wash it off immediately.

Book Strand

Book strand 3, Designing with Shapes and Objects, includes this lesson in its diagram, pictured below. See page xiv for a complete description of this strand.

Designing with Shapes and Objects

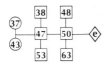

LESSON 39

Drawing Distortions

Suggested Art Materials

See the art materials list for this lesson in the student book.

Planning Ahead

If a rounded or curved mirror is available, have students look at themselves and objects in the classroom to better understand the concept of distortion.
Additional Materials Needed:
rounded mirror

Helpful Teaching Hints

• When students are preparing the second grid with curved lines, suggest that they repeat the same curved line both vertically and horizontally on their paper.
• Have students study the work of fine artists, such as Picasso, who used distortion. Discuss how Cubism as an art style evolved and how Cubist artists used distortion in their work.

Book Strand

Book strand 13, Fantasy and Distortion, includes this lesson in its diagram, pictured below. See page xv for a complete description of this strand.

Fantasy and Distortion

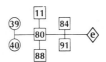

LESSON 40

Slice, Twist, and Stretch

Suggested Art Materials

See the art materials list for this lesson in the student book.

Helpful Teaching Hints

For less mess, use cotton swabs to apply glue to small pieces of design.
Additional Materials Needed:
cotton swabs

Safety Precautions

Use glue only in a well-ventilated area.

Book Strand

Book strand 13, Fantasy and Distortion, includes this lesson in its diagram, pictured below. See page xv for a complete description of this strand.

Fantasy and Distortion

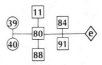

LESSON 41

Creating with Stitches

Suggested Art Materials

See the art materials list for this lesson in the student book.

Planning Ahead

Start collecting a variety of fabrics, yarns, buttons, and other found objects. Ask the students to help build this collection, too.

Helpful Teaching Hints

Keep small objects, buttons, etc., in labeled jars, so they can be easily found when needed.

Additional Materials Needed:
jars, labels

Safety Precautions

Pull needles through fabric slowly and carefully, moving them away from face and body.

Book Strand

Book strand 4, Surfaces and Textures, includes this lesson in its diagram, pictured at the top of the following page. See page xiv for a complete description of this strand.

Surfaces and Textures

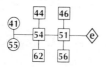

LESSON 42

Geometry with a Needle

Suggested Art Materials

See the art materials list for this lesson in the student book.

Planning Ahead

Procure rug or tapestry backing, or use plastic window screening for background.

Helpful Teaching Hints

Demonstrate the stitches to be used. If the fabric is too loose to hold a knot, backstitch to hold the thread in place.

Safety Precautions

Pull needles through slowly and carefully, moving them away from face and body.

Book Strand

Book strand 2, Creating with Lines, includes this lesson in its diagram, pictured below. See page xiii for a complete description of this strand.

Creating with Lines

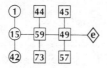

LESSON 43

Pictures in Cloth

Suggested Art Materials

See the art materials list for this lesson in the student book.

Planning Ahead

Have plenty of differently colored—patterned and plain—fabrics on hand to choose from. All-cotton is best because the edges are less likely to ravel, and the finished product will be washable.

Helpful Teaching Hints

Make muslin tubes to sew onto the backs of wall hangings: slip dowels inside, put screw eyes on the ends of the dowels, and hang by twine or wire.
Additional Materials Needed:
muslin, dowels, screw eyes, twine or wire

Safety Precautions

Pull needles through slowly and carefully, moving them away from face and body.

Book Strand

Book strand 3, Designing with Shapes and Objects, and book strand 15, Learning About Shape, include this lesson in their diagrams, pictured below. See pages xiv and xv for a complete description of these strands.

Designing with
Shapes and Objects   Learning About Shape

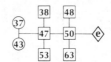   

LESSON 44

Weaving on a Natural Loom

Suggested Art Materials

See the art materials list for this lesson in the student book.

Planning Ahead

Prepare a sample of off-loom weaving, and/or show examples in reproductions, slides, or films, so students may see possibilities for design in this craft.

Helpful Teaching Hints

- Slightly green wood is best to use, as older branches may be too dried out and will break when warp threads are tightened.
- In making the warp, do not merely wind string around the arms of the branch. Instead, wind over one arm, then under and over the opposite arm. This provides a tighter warp which will not stretch as easily when worked.

Book Strands

Book strand 2, Creating with Lines, and book strand 4, Surfaces and Textures, include this lesson in their diagrams, pictured below. See pages xiii and xiv, respectively, for complete descriptions of these strands.

Creating with Lines   Surfaces and Textures

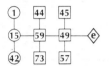 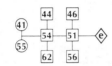

LESSON 45

The Art of Macramé

Suggested Art Materials

See the art materials list for this lesson in the student book.

Planning Ahead

Prepare materials giving the history of macramé. (It was much practiced by sailors in the 19th and early 20th centuries. Early examples are shown in museums.)

Helpful Teaching Hints

- Encourage the students to choose simple projects to begin with, as macramé can become complex and tedious.
- Students may be interested in doing macramé earrings, jewelry, or plant hangers. Hobby shops carry directions for these.

Book Strand

Book strand 2, Creating with Lines, includes this lesson in its diagram, pictured below. See page xiii for a complete description of this strand.

Creating with Lines

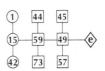

Planning Ahead

Have the students participate in assembling a collection of small, lightweight objects that could be drilled or used as beads. Strive for variety in shape, color, and texture.

Helpful Teaching Hints

- Keep bead materials in plastic desk organizers or similar containers.*
- Demonstrate the correct use of the drill and hammer. Insist on safety.
- Encourage students to lay out their beads in various arrangements, trying out several designs, before stringing.

Additional Materials Needed:
* small containers

Safety Precautions

Students should wear safety goggles and work only in designated areas when using tools. Small objects can fly up and injure eyes.

Use shellac and paint thinner only in a well-ventilated area.

Book Strand

Book strand 4, Surfaces and Textures, includes this lesson in its diagram, pictured below. See page xiv for a complete description of this strand.

Surfaces and Textures

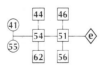

LESSON 46

Creativity with Beads

Suggested Art Materials

See the art materials list in the student book.

Planning Ahead

Have the students participate in assembling a collection of small, lightweight objects that could be drilled or used as beads. Strive for variety in shape, color, and texture.

Helpful Teaching Hints

- Keep bead materials in plastic desk organizers or similar containers.*
- Demonstrate the correct use of the drill and hammer. Insist on safety.
- Encourage students to lay out their beads in various arrangements, trying out several designs, before stringing.

Additional Materials Needed.
* small containers

Safety Precautions

Students should wear safety goggles and work only in designated areas when using tools. Small objects can fly up and injure eyes.

Use shellac and paint thinner only in a well-ventilated area.

Book Strands

Book strand 4, Surfaces and Textures, includes this lesson in its diagram, pictured below. See page ix for a complete description of this strand.

Surfaces and Textures

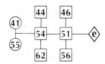

LESSON 47

Printmaking with Linoleum Blocks

Suggested Art Materials

See the art materials list in the student book.

Planning Ahead

Collect reproductions of block printing, both historic and contemporary. Most major artists, past and present, have tried their hands at woodcuts or some other form of block printing. Choose simple designs and motifs to show.

Helpful Teaching Hints

Demonstrate the correct use of linoleum cutting tools.

Safety Precautions

Tools need to be sharp to do the job well. Insist on safe use (cut away from the body and keep fingers out of the cutting path). Keep tools in slotted or divided containers when not in use.

Book Strand

Book strand 3, Designing with Shapes and Objects, includes this lesson in its diagram, pictured on the following page. See page xiv for a complete description of this strand.

Designing with Shapes and Objects

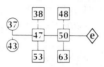

LESSON 48

Visual Word Messages

Suggested Art Materials

See the art materials list for this lesson in the student book.

Planning Ahead

Have on hand many examples of words for students to choose from. Show books of different lettering designs (available from typesetting firms).

Helpful Teaching Hints

- Point out that the choice of colors is very important, as colors also reflect moods.
- Ask the students to find pictures of the items or feelings represented by their words. Use these to discuss how important it is for artists to reveal their own interpretations of the real world through their creative efforts.

Safety Precautions

If the students use India ink, remind them of its permanence. If it gets on the skin, wash it off immediately.

Book Strand

Book strand 3, Designing with Shapes and Objects, includes this lesson in its diagram, pictured below. See page xiv for a complete description of this strand.

Designing with Shapes and Objects

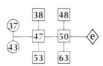

LESSON 49

Drawing Letter Shapes

Suggested Art Materials

See the art materials list in the student book.

Helpful Teaching Hints

- Demonstrate the use of lettering pens, or ask a professional graphic artist or calligrapher to demonstrate their use.
- Use pre-lined or grid paper for this lesson.*

Additional Materials Needed:
* pre-lined or grid paper

Safety Precautions

If the students use India ink, remind them of its permanency. If it gets on the skin, wash it off immediately.

Book Strand

Book strand 2, Creating with Lines, and book strand 17, Relationships in Design, include this lesson in their diagrams, pictured below. See pages xiii and xvi for a complete description of this strand.

Creating with Lines   Relationships in Design

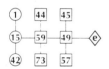   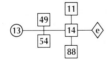

LESSON 50

Designing a Poster

Suggested Art Materials

See the art materials list in the student book.

Planning Ahead

You may want to coordinate this lesson with a major campaign—anti-drunk driving, heart disease, a community event, school carnival, school play—or yearly poster competitions.

Helpful Teaching Hints

- Emphasize unity of composition, balance of form and color, and impact of message.
- For inspiration, collect and exhibit posters with good design qualities. Discuss with students the merits of each.

Related Art Career (commercial artist)

Commercial artist, or designer, is a broad job title encompassing several specific careers in the field of applied arts, or art put to practical use. Detailed information on some of these can be found in the following lessons: graphic designer, Lesson 5; book illustrator, Lesson 35; scientific illustrator, Lesson 6; and industrial designer, Lesson 89. Ask students to think of other job titles that might be included in the field of commercial art.

Book Strand

Book strand 3, Designing with Shapes and Objects, includes this lesson in its diagram, pictured below. See page xiv for a complete description of this strand.

Designing with Shapes and Objects

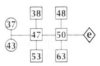

Exploring Art

Advertising Books, Movies, and Music

See page 24 for an explanation and teaching suggestions.

Unit IV
Modeling, Carving, and Construction

Learning Objectives

In this unit, the student will achieve the following objectives:

Understanding Art

- Understand that three-dimensional artworks look different when the angle at which they are viewed changes
- Understand the importance of tactile qualities in three-dimensional artworks
- Understand the properties of clay and the three basic methods of creating pottery
- Recognize the use of proportion, scale, and balance in sculpture

Creating Art

- Create balanced three-dimensional artworks
- Use clay for modeling and for creating pottery and sculpture
- Use a variety of tools to create textures on clay
- Create pottery, using the three basic methods
- Incorporate space into sculptures
- Create several types of sculpture out of many different materials

Appreciating Art

- Recognize and appreciate basic trends and styles in sculpture
- Appreciate the beauty of artworks made from everyday objects
- Derive satisfaction from working with clay

Unit Strands

A strand consists of a group of related lessons where the student is expected to begin with one of the lesson choices available on the far left (arranged vertically), complete it, proceed horizontally to the next group of choices, make a choice and complete the lesson, and so forth, until the entire sequence has been completed. (See page v for complete instructions on using strands.) The unit strands for this unit are diagrammed at the top of the next column.

Strand H: Reliefs, Sculpture, and Ceramics

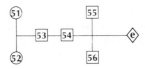

Strand I: Sculpting, Modeling, and Carving

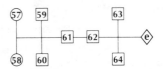

Background Information

Unit IV is designed to provide the students with experience in and knowledge of three-dimensional art forms. Through exposure to modeling, carving, and construction, students come to recognize and appreciate three-dimensional art forms found in the environment. The students also develop a sense of form and space—something which the two-dimensional effect of painting and drawing cannot provide except through illusion.

Throughout this unit, the students are encouraged to use their senses. The sense of touch is very important to those lessons which are centered on creating textural effects—the early lessons on relief and the introductory lessons on using clay, for example. And the sense of sight is especially important to lessons 57 and 58, which stress balance in art. All the senses must work together in the advanced sculpting lessons. These lessons require visualization, a keen sense of balance and proportion, and manual dexterity in the handling of tools. The students will work best when completing these lessons (lessons 59–63) if distractions are kept to a minimum.

The last lesson in the unit, The Sculpture of Henry Moore, follows the principle behind this book which stresses the importance of exposing students to well-known artworks. Other important sculptors, such as Alexander Calder, are also introduced within the unit. Additionally, ancient examples of pottery and other functional art pieces are shown, affirming for the students the continuing importance of art in the history of mankind. All of these samples should serve to stimulate and challenge the students, giving them the incentive to create their own artworks of merit.

Strategies for Motivation

Students are usually more motivated in art classes if they can relate what they are doing with what they see around them. Especially for this unit, which stresses art which is decorative *and* functional, the students must learn to find the art in their environment. The following suggestions will motivate them towards artistic interpretations of three-dimensional forms in the everyday environment.

- Show pictures of famous sculptures which appear in front of buildings or within parks. Discuss whether or not these sculptures are applicable to their settings, or have the students try to guess in what types of surroundings these artworks are located.
- Ask the students to take note of all the three-dimensional forms they encounter between school and home; have them tell about these forms, relating them to their surroundings and discussing their merits.
- Discuss three-dimensional works in terms of their reality as well as their abstraction from natural forms.

Extending Art

Exploring Art

The Exploring Art feature for Unit IV extends art beyond the classroom by instructing each student to design a sculpture for an outdoor area. Sculptures are to fit in with their surroundings, and students are to construct small-scale models of their sculptures. Begin by discussing the examples of outdoor sculpture shown in the student book and in other illustrations you provide. Ask students how the features of the sculptures (size, shape, materials) make them appropriate to their surroundings. Direct students to take these features into account when designing their own sculptures. Further extensions of this lesson include the following:

- Assign students to create designs for playground sculptures meant to be touched and climbed on, as well as to function as art. Materials used should be practical, safe, and available (wood, pipes, tires, rope, etc.). If appropriate, students can work in groups of five or six to actually build their sculptures and donate them to a preschool or playground.

- Have students research sculptors who create large outdoor sculptures. Each student can choose a sculptor whose style he or she likes and create a design based on this style. The student's model could then be displayed next to a photo of the favored sculptor's work.

Additional Activities

Visits to museums and art galleries are common sources of reinforcement of the knowledge gained in the classroom. Follow such visits with discussions of the three-dimensional works viewed. Particularly emphasizing the different types of media used will provide the students with better insight into the creation of three-dimensional art forms. Other suggestions for additional activities follow.

- Take field trips to community centers, parks, and other places in your area where sculptures are displayed. Discuss these artworks in terms of style, media used, and surroundings.
- Ask students to turn in written reports on their favorite sculptors, or have them give oral reports of individual excursions to art displays.

Evaluating Procedures

As noted in the introduction to this book, evaluation in art classes poses unique problems for the teacher. (See pages vii-viii.) The Learning Outcomes address the need for self-evaluation and test the students on the details of what they have learned. However, the teacher still needs some means of determining the extent of a student's application of specifics to a solid core of basic art knowledge. Three things are involved in this type of evaluation:

1. A written test of the student's recall of important facts
2. An examination of the student's artwork in terms of the achievement of certain previously stated goals
3. An oral discussion with the student involving his or her comments on a particular piece of art

These three evaluative components for Unit IV are explained below.

Vocabulary

Students who complete this unit should be able to define and correctly use the art terms listed below and on the following page. A written test on the unit should, then, be based on these terms.

abstract	module
additive sculpture	perceive
asymmetry	pinch method

balanced
bronze
cast
ceramics
coil method
contour
embossing
fire
found objects
fourth dimension
grain
intersected
kiln
kinetic sculpture
lacquer
medium
mobile

piane
portrait
proportions
relief
replica
scale
slab method
small-scale
style
subtractive sculpture
symmetry
texture
three-dimensional
unified
visualizing
voids

Skills

The artworks students complete in this unit should meet the standards listed below. Be certain that the students are aware of these standards both as they plan and as they work. You may choose to keep this list posted throughout the time spent on this unit.

- The artwork looks balanced and unified from all angles.
- The artwork reveals knowledge of how the parts and planes fit together and of how space functions as a part of the structure.

Application of Knowledge

Listening to a student talk about an artwork can give you a true sense of how much the student understands the basic elements and principles of design. However, the planning behind such a discussion is important. First, the work to be discussed must be chosen in advance by the teacher. Questions must be written that will lead the student into the correct areas of emphasis. Last, the discussion should be arranged to take place on a one-to-one basis so the more reticent students are not left out of a group discussion.

A suggested artwork to use for discussion purposes in this unit is the sculpture by Frank Dobson entitled *Two Heads.*

Supplementary Materials and Resources

Baker, Leslie A. *The Art Teacher's Resource Book.* Reston, Va.: Reston Publishing Co., Inc., 1979.
This is a useful resource book which includes, besides information on other areas of art, information on ceramics, construction, carving, and

casting. Diversified and interesting suggestions about art experiences suitable for the classroom provide the teacher with many options.

Beginning Ceramics. Modesto, Calif.: Nasco Arts and Crafts, 1984. Slides.
This complete slide unit is composed of three parts. Part I depicts clay preparation and the making of a balloon pot from two petal pots. Part II shows the procedures for making a pinch pot and for making a coil constructed pot. Part III directs viewers through the necessary steps for forming a pitcher out of clay slabs, attaching a handle and a spout, and glazing the final product.

Nigrosh, Leong I. *Claywork—Form and Idea in Ceramic Design.* Worcester, Mass.: Davis Publications, Inc., 1984.
This comprehensive, easy-to-use guide to working with clay provides detailed coverage to answer the needs of students, teachers, and both beginning and experienced potters. Slab, pinch, coil, and throwing methods are discussed with historical and contemporary examples used to suggest design possibilities for each method. Numerous ways to add textural and decorative details are given, and all techniques are supported by clear photographs depicting each step.

Reed, Carl and Joseph Orze. *Art from Scrap.* Worcester, Mass.: Books for Art Education, 1984.
This book is an invitation to explore and utilize found objects and recycled materials, related to contemporary living, in the creation of three-dimensional art forms.

TEACHING SUGGESTIONS for Lessons 51–64

LESSON 51

Embossing Shining Images

Suggested Art Materials

See the art materials list for this lesson in the student book.

Planning Ahead

Bring in actual examples of embossed leather and metal. Pass these around for your students to handle and feel.

Helpful Teaching Hints

- Encourage the students to plan their designs carefully on paper. Remind them that simple lines will work best for their reliefs.
- Ball point pens are the most effective tools to use in this lesson for drawing the lines and pushing out the relief areas.

Safety Precautions

Remind the students that India ink can be permanent. Have the students wash their skin immediately if the easily-absorbed ink or the harsh lacquer is contacted. Use glue and lacquer in well-ventilated areas only.

Book Strand

Book strand 4, Surfaces and Textures, includes this lesson in its diagram, pictured below. See page xiv for a complete description of this strand.

Surfaces and Textures

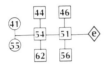

LESSON 52

Relief Sculpture

Suggested Art Materials

See the art materials list in the student book.

Planning Ahead

Tell students in advance to collect disposable objects whose shapes and textures are interesting to them.

Helpful Teaching Hints

Have the students first create a relief based on symmetrical balance before attempting to achieve asymmetrical balance.

Safety Precaution

Use glue only in a well-ventilated area.

Book Strand

Book strand 14, The Road to Abstraction, includes this lesson in its diagram, pictured at the top of the next column. See page xv for a complete description of this strand.

The Road to Abstraction

LESSON 53

Bricks and Beehives

Suggested Art Materials

See the art materials list for this lesson in the student book.

Planning Ahead

Prepare for the lesson by using matchboxes or building blocks to create a modular sculpture. Then use your students' suggestions to rearrange the parts in various ways.

Helpful Teaching Hints

Extend the discussion of what makes a modular sculpture effective by talking about the sculptures pictured in the student text. How would the students change these to make them better?

Safety Precautions

Use glue and spray paints only in a well-ventilated area. If you cannot go outside to use the spray paints, have large boxes on hand. The students can place the objects in these boxes during spraying.

Book Strand

Book strand 3, Designing with Shapes and Objects, includes this lesson in its diagram, pictured below. See page xiv for a complete description of this strand.

Designing with Shapes and Objects

LESSON 54

Descriptive Modeling

Suggested Art Materials

See the art materials list for this lesson in the student book.

Helpful Teaching Hints

- Ask your students to bring in any miniatures they might have: model cars, doll house furnishings, souvenirs, etc. Discuss each of these objects in terms of its validity as a model for the real-life object.
- Have the students draw sketches of the objects they intend to create models of. Ask the students to work in small groups to discuss the sketches. Are correct proportions used? Are any of the details going to be too hard to create in clay?
- Finished clay pieces should be allowed to dry naturally and completely for several days in a warm place until they no longer feel cold to the touch.
- If the clay is to be fired, be aware that the firing temperature required to mature various types of clay differs. You should select clay and glazes that mature at the same temperature—which may be determined by the capability of your kiln.
- Firing is a two-stage process. Dried clay (sometimes known as "greenware") may be stacked and loaded as closely and tightly as possible for the first firing. This firing will be to approximately cone 015, or 1,500°F, and will bring the clay to a "bisque" stage where it is halfway matured, but still porous enough to absorb liquid glaze.
- Coat the base or foot of bisque ware with commercial *wax resist* or melted paraffin, or simply avoid getting glaze on areas that will touch the kiln shelf. Bisque ware may be glazed either by dipping or pouring the glaze on, or by evenly painting on three coats with a soft brush. Glazed pieces must be loaded into the kiln carefully so they do not touch anything.

Safety Precautions

- Typical firing temperatures for "high fire" clay bodies range from 2,000 to 2,200°F—VERY HOT! A firing kiln should always be supervised to make sure it is operating properly and shuts off when visible "cones" placed in the viewer windows have bent over to indicate that the required temperature has been reached. Students should not be allowed near a hot kiln: clothing can easily be ignited if it touches the kiln, and serious burns are a potential hazard.
- A fired kiln should be allowed to cool naturally for 16 to 24 hours, and should never be opened before it has cooled below at least 500°F. Impatience on this count will result in crazing, tiny networks of cracks in the glaze and clay, which can cause pots to leak or break.

- If you and/or your equipment and materials are new, some experimenting is advisable to discover the most successful combinations of clay types; glaze colors, brands, or formulas; and firing techniques. What takes place inside a firing kiln is really a complicated set of chemical reactions, and because of the large number of variables, some clay bodies will accept some glazes better than others. Glazes may turn out quite differently if fired in a gas or electric kiln; and slight differences in firing temperatures may produce very different effects.

Book Strand

Book strand 4, Surfaces and Textures, includes this lesson in its diagram, pictured below. See page xiv for a complete description of this strand.

Surfaces and Textures

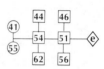

LESSON 55

Fancy Pottery

Suggested Art Materials

See the art materials list in the student book.

Planning Ahead

Allow several class periods for this lesson. That way, students can experiment with each of the methods of creating pottery.

Helpful Teaching Hints

- Have the students simply create pottery using each method, without worrying about decorating the pieces. Once each student decides which method is preferred, he or she can then create an elaborate piece of pottery, using this method.
- See Lesson 54 for instructions on drying, firing, and glazing pottery.
- Arrange a display of the students' final pieces. Ask each student to title the piece and to describe it on an index card to be placed next to the piece.*

Additional Materials Needed:
* materials for display, index cards

Safety Precautions

When using sharp tools, always cut away from the fingers and body. Remind the students of the rules for using a kiln. (See the previous lesson guide).

Related Art Career (potter)

In past civilizations the potter's main purpose was to create functional, everyday items. Today these are inexpensively mass-produced, so the potter as craftsman (one who creates with skill of the hands) has turned toward the creation of unique fine art, decorative items.

Basic art education at a college or art school is a good foundation for this career. Knowledge of the craft, its materials, and tools can also be gained through specialty classes or practical experience.

Many potters market their artwork through craft and trade shows. They often join a craft organization through which their work is exhibited at local or regional malls or sidewalk shows. Some also combine their time and resources to operate cooperative centers. Because these types of business operations require financial expenditures before items are sold, potters will often turn to teaching their specialty at adult or community centers for extra income.

Have students attend a local craft show or a pottery display in a museum. Conduct a class discussion comparing present day uses and styles of pottery with the functional pieces of the past. If possible, have a local potter-craftsman visit the class, discuss his or her specialty, and give a demonstration.

Book Strand

Book strand 4, Surfaces and Textures, includes this lesson in its diagram, pictured below. See page xiv for a complete description of this strand.

Surfaces and Textures

LESSON 56

Three-Legged Pottery

Suggested Art Materials

See the art materials list in the student book.

Helpful Teaching Hints

- Begin this lesson with a discussion of design as complementing function. Ask the students to name functional pieces of artwork they have seen in modern homes.
- Ask the students to choose a different method of creating pottery than those used previously.

- See Lesson 54 for instructions on drying, firing, and glazing.

Safety Precautions

See this section in Lessons 54 and 55.

Book Strand

Book strand 4, Surfaces and Textures, includes this lesson in its diagram, pictured below. See page xiv for a complete description of this strand.

Surfaces and Textures

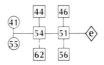

LESSON 57

Sculpting with String

Suggested Art Materials

See the art materials list in the student book.

Planning Ahead

Prepare some sheets of plywood for the students to use in this lesson. Nail upholstery tacks to the boards in a variety of patterns.

Helpful Teaching Hints

Let the students experiment with string or wire, using your prepared boards. They can then create their own arrangements of tacks on other sheets of plywood.

Safety Precautions

- Keep nails and tacks in labeled boxes.
- If possible, have the students wear gloves when working with wire.
- Make small, tapping motions when using a hammer.

Book Strand

Book strand 2, Creating with Lines, includes this lesson in its diagram, pictured below. See page xiii for a complete description of this strand.

Creating with Lines

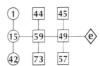

LESSON 58

Art That Balances

Suggested Art Materials

See the art materials list in the student book.

Helpful Teaching Hints

Show the students how to find the *fulcrum*, or balancing point, using a stick with a weight hanging at either end. Stress that the fulcrum is important to understand and achieve when creating mobiles.

Safety Precaution

Wear gloves when working with wire and wire cutters.

Book Strand

Book strand 11, Learning from Artists, includes this lesson in its diagram, pictured below. See page xv for a complete description of this strand.

Learning from Artists

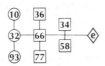

LESSON 59

Sculpting with Lines

Suggested Art Materials

See the art materials list for this lesson in the student book.

Planning Ahead

Get several feet of many types of wire from a hardware store.

Helpful Teaching Hints

• Discuss the properties of the various types of wire—pliability, strength, etc.—and how these properties do or do not lend themselves to particular designs.
• Ask the students to sketch the designs they wish to create. The students can decide, based on these sketches, which type of wire is best for each design.

Safety Precaution

If possible, have the students wear gloves when working with wire.

Book Strand

Book strand 2, Creating with Lines, includes this lesson in its diagram, pictured below. See page xiii for a complete description of this strand.

Creating with Lines

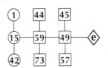

LESSON 60

Skeleton Sculpture

Suggested Art Materials

See the art materials list for this lesson in the student book.

Helpful Teaching Hints

Students will enjoy adding realistic details to their sculptures: bits of fabric for clothes, straw or yarn for hair, etc.
Additional Materials Needed:
fabric scraps, buttons, straw, etc.

Safety Precautions

When using sharp tools, always cut *away* from the body and keep fingers out of the path.

Book Strands

Book strand 10, Visions and Feelings, and book strand 12, Studying People, include this lesson in their diagrams, pictured below. See page xv for complete descriptions of these strands.

Visions and Feelings   Studying People

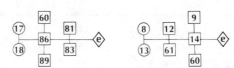

LESSON 61

Portrait in Clay

Suggested Art Materials

See the art materials list for this lesson in the student book.

Helpful Teaching Hints

- Refer the students to Lesson 8, in which the correct proportions for drawing a head are discussed.
- Have spray bottles filled with water available for the students' use (to keep the clay moist).*
- Once the sculpted heads are dry, have the students paint on the details of eyes, cheeks, lips, etc.**

Additional Materials Needed:
  * spray bottles
** paints and brushes

Safety Precautions

When using sharp tools, always cut *away* from the body and keep fingers out of the path.

Book Strand

Book strand 12, Studying People, includes this lesson in its diagram, pictured below. See page xv for a complete description of this strand.

Studying People

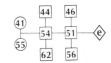

LESSON 62

Hand Sculpture

Suggested Art Materials

See the art materials list for this lesson in the student book.

Helpful Teaching Hints

- Discuss the properties of each suggested art material. Have each student handle the materials, decide which one is preferable, and then draw a sketch for a sculpture which would complement the material chosen.
- Remind the students that they should choose a style of sculpting which they prefer—whether it be a style that uses only smooth and simplified planes, or a style that really exploits textural qualities and decoration.

Safety Precautions

- Remind the students to have dry hands when using carving tools and to cut away from the body, keeping fingers out of the cutting path.
- If glazes are used, be sure the ventilation is ade-

quate. Have the students wash any of these products off the skin immediately.

Book Strands

Book strand 4, Surfaces and Textures, and book strand 14, The Road to Abstraction, include this lesson in their diagrams, pictured below. See pages xiv and xv, respectively, for complete descriptions of these strands.

Surfaces and Textures   The Road to Abstraction

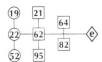

LESSON 63

Abstract Carving

Suggested Art Materials

See the art materials list in the student book.

Planning Ahead

You can create plaster blocks by pouring liquid plaster into cardboard cartons. The cardboard can be removed when the plaster hardens.
Additional Materials Needed:
cardboard cartons

Helpful Teaching Hints

Urge the students to spend the majority of their time working on the main forms and planes of their sculptures. Stress that details are not important in abstract sculpture. It is the form that provides the aesthetic value of the sculpture.

Safety Precautions

Remind the students to carve away from the body and to keep fingers out of the cutting path.

Book Strand

Book strand 3, Designing with Shapes and Objects, includes this lesson in its diagram, pictured below. See page xiv for a complete description of this strand.

Designing with Shapes and Objects

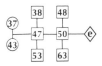

LESSON 64

The Sculpture of Henry Moore

Suggested Art Materials

See the art materials list in the student book.

Helpful Teaching Hints

- Ask a student to give an oral report on Henry Moore.
- Show as many examples as possible of Henry Moore's work. Discuss each in terms of the properties outlined in the student text.*

Additional Materials Needed:

* pictures, slides, other visuals showing Moore's work

Safety Precautions

Remind the students to carve away from the body and to keep fingers out of the cutting path.

Related Art Career (sculptor)

Whether sculpted in a monumental, realistic style reminiscent of Michelangelo, or in a smooth, touchable, abstract style like the work of Henry Moore, sculpture is experiencing renewed popularity today.

A sculptor may be commissioned to create an artwork for the interiors of public buildings, such as libraries, banks, malls, and other commercial places, as well as outdoor areas surrounding these buildings.

The architectural sculptor needs an awareness of people and a knowledge of interior and exterior space, in addition to an interest in architecture. A representative usually handles the business details, but the sculptor should be knowledgeable in this area and also understand the logistics of handling, delivering, and installing large pieces of artwork.

Ask students to observe pieces of sculpture in their community. Discuss the techniques, styles, and media employed by the sculptors. Also discuss how the pieces of sculpture harmonize with their respective environments.

Book Strand

Book strand 14, The Road to Abstraction, includes this lesson in its diagram, pictured below. See page xv for a complete description of this strand.

The Road to Abstraction

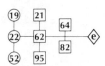

Exploring Art

A Sculpture for Outdoors

See page 33 for an explanation and teaching suggestions.

Unit V
Art in the Environment

Learning Objectives

In this unit, the students will achieve the following objectives:

Understanding Art

- Understand art as both a portrayal of the world around us and as inherent therein
- Understand the role of visual memory in the creation of art
- Identify the architectural styles of the important cultures throughout history
- Understand and discuss how buildings and bridges are supported

Creating Art

- Draw buildings representative of many architectural styles
- Use details and setting in drawings, to complement an architectural style
- Build models according to plans

Appreciating Art

- Appreciate artworks in the built environment as linking form to purpose
- Recognize noted architects' styles and appreciate their special properties
- Appreciate the role of art in architecture throughout history
- Appreciate the way the environment, natural or man-made, can complement art forms

Unit Strands

A strand consists of a group of related lessons where the student is expected to begin with one of the lesson choices available on the far left (arranged vertically), complete it, proceed horizontally to the next group of choices, make a choice and complete the lesson, and so forth, until the entire sequence has been completed. (See page v-vi for complete instructions on using strands.) The unit strands for this unit are diagramed as follows:

Strand J: Studying Places and Buildings

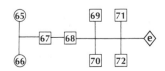

Strand K: Styles of Architecture

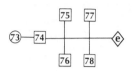

Background Information

We live in a built environment. Art is part of it—in the forms of buildings, landscapes, sculptures, and other elements of environmental design. Art helps to beautify the environment by creating pleasant living spaces. In this unit students learn to see environmental art in their surroundings. They also study architecture of the past and of the present. The knowledge the students gain helps them to appreciate their surroundings and to develop an understanding that the designs of objects and structures, the layouts of cities and towns, and the natural landscape all affect our way of life.

Since environmental art is a very large and extensive area of study, this unit does not ask students to become involved in elaborate and highly technical projects. Rather, the thrust of the unit is reduced to one important idea: the students are provided with an awareness of their environment—an awareness that appreciates the harmonious blending of the natural and the man-made. Thus, the actual lessons that students must do first provide the students with knowledge of styles and the reasons behind them and then ask the students to make aesthetic judgments, both practical and decorative, about their own portrayals of the built and natural environment.

The first lesson in the unit, Farms and Plantations, immediately makes the students aware of the important role of the natural environment. The next three lessons build on the interplay between natural and man-made objects by juxtaposing the Wild West, New York City, and places the students themselves are familiar with. Immediately, then, the students get a feel for how many types of environments there are. Correspondingly, a sense of form as related to function emerges. The students, asked to use their visual memories, really begin to notice their own environment.

The remainder of the lessons take the students on a historical tour of architecture, from ancient Greece and Rome through modern times. The reasons for particular architectural details are discussed, and ample examples of each style are given. The students then incorporate elements of these designs into their own artworks. They learn to blend buildings into the environment. They learn to respect the styles of other times and cultures as practical and beautiful. They also learn why and how modern structures look the way they do. In short, the students' eyes are opened to the beauty that is inherent in their surroundings—whether they be rural or urban, old-fashioned or modern.

Strategies for Motivation

The concept of art as part of the environment is an important one. It has to do with our living conditions and is vital to our well-being. In this unit, then, it is necessary to always refer to the students' immediate surroundings. Relating the lessons to the students' own living environments in addition to the rather exotic environments of some of the pictured buildings will make this unit a more realistic experience. Following are some suggestions along these lines.

- Take lots of photographs, from all angles, of buildings that are important in your area. Display these photographs, and have the students point out details that stem from the styles they are studying.
- Have the students, as a class project, design and build a model school. This activity will help them to understand the importance of planning and of incorporating functional architectural details. Let them be as imaginative as possible when designing the school, but caution them that the style must fit into the environment. You might even have the students choose a local site where their school would be built.
- Have a local architect bring blueprints for a building to show and discuss in class. It would be especially effective to see the blueprints of an already built building and then actually go see the results.
- Have students who live in older homes tell about the unique features of these houses; students living in ultra-modern structures could do the same.

Extending Art

Exploring Art

This Exploring Art feature relates art to such career fields as architecture and city planning, by directing students to design buildings compatible with those in a given area of the community. Each student's design is to take into account the purpose for which the new building will be used. Before students begin work, supply copies of such magazines as *Architectural Digest*, and discuss the ways that the structures shown complement their surroundings. Ask students to point out examples of form following function. To further extend this lesson:

- Assign students to make scale models of the buildings they have sketched or photographed. Or, as an alternative, assign students to make scale models of famous structures in other areas or from other time periods (Stonehenge, the Pyramids, the World Trade Center). Students can work from art and photos in books and periodicals.
- Let the class work as a group to create a scale model of your school neighborhood or your city center. They will need to refer to maps and/or aerial photographs, as well as their own drawings and snapshots, as they work. The finished model can be displayed in a central area of the school.

Additional Activities

Learning from first-hand experience is most appropriate and easy where art and the environment is concerned, since an immediate and ready-made set of examples is available in the surroundings. Following are some suggestions for taking advantage of these examples.

- Take a walk around the area of your school, pointing out and discussing architecture and the natural environment. If possible, extend the walk to compare and contrast the architecture found along a waterfront, in the countryside, and in urban areas.
- Explore with your class different gardens and parks in your area. Then have the students create their own bottle gardens or design, on paper, gardens and parks to complement the buildings they draw in the lessons.
- As a class, create a mural that depicts your town. The mural should include buildings, landscapes, and other environmental art. Each student can depict his or her own home on the mural.

Evaluating Procedures

As noted in the introduction to this book, evaluation in art classes poses unique problems for the teacher. (See pages vii-viii.) The *Learning Outcomes* address the need for self-evaluation and test the students on the details of what they have learned. However, the teacher still needs some means of determining the extent of a student's application of specifics to a solid core of basic art knowledge. Three things are involved in this type of evaluation:

1. A written test of the student's recall of important facts
2. An examination of the student's artwork in terms of the achievement of certain previously stated goals
3. An oral discussion with the student involving his or her comments on a particular piece of art.

These three evaluative components for Unit V are explained below.

Vocabulary

Students who complete this unit should be able to define and correctly use the art terms listed below. A written test on the unit should, then, be based on these terms.

abstract	modular
arch	Parthenon
Baroque	pediment
beam	plan
column	polyhedron
dome	portico
foreground	post
fortress	pyramid
frieze	realistic
geodesic dome	sketch
girder	skyscraper
Gothic	summit
lintel	suspension
medium	symbolic ornamentation
Middle Ages	vault
moat	visual memory

Skills

The artworks students create in this unit should meet the standards listed below. Be certain that the students are aware of these standards both as they plan and as they work. You may choose to keep this list posted throughout the time spent on this unit.

• The details of the building are appropriate to the style of architecture.
• The details of the building's environment complement the style of the building.
• The model follows a definite plan and is sturdily constructed.
• Correct scale and proportion are employed.

Application of Knowledge

Listening to a student talk about an artwork can give

you a true sense of how much the student understands the basic elements and principles of design. However, the planning behind such a discussion is important. First, the work to be discussed must be chosen in advance and studied by the teacher. Questions must be written that will lead the student into the correct areas of emphasis. Last, the discussion should be arranged to take place on a one-to-one basis so that the more reticent students are not left out of a group discussion.

A suggested artwork to use for discussion purposes in this unit is the modern structure entitled *Habitat*, designed by Moshe Safdie and located in Montreal.

Supplementary Materials and Resources

Teacher Resources

Brommer, Gerald F. *Drawing—Ideas, Materials, Techniques.* Worcester, MA: Books for Art Education, 1978.
Organized to provide maximum flexibility, this book looks at the act of drawing. Part I covers drawing media, tools, and techniques. Part II focuses on subject matter—figures, landscapes, still lifes, architecture, abstraction, and more.

Student Resources

Hillyer, V.M. and E.G. Huey. *Young People's Story of Architecture.* New York: Meredith Press, 1966.
This book is an invaluable visual aid. It gives examples of Egyptian, Roman, and early Christian architecture, all supplemented by simple text.

TEACHING SUGGESTIONS
for Lessons 65–78

LESSON 65

Farms and Plantations

Suggested Art Materials

See the art materials list in the student book.

Planning Ahead

If at all possible, plan a trip to the country, or even the suburbs, as a preface to the lesson. Ask the students to bring along their sketchbooks and to spend the time, in the country alone, sketching scenes of nature and relishing the lack of artificial surroundings. They can then use their visual memories when back in the classroom drawing landscapes.

Helpful Teaching Hints

- Refer the students to lessons 16 and 17 (on perspective) in Unit I. Also remind them of the ways to use color in order to show distance.
- Urge the students to fill their sketchbooks with any environmental art they encounter while studying this unit. By doing so, they will build a helpful "visual vocabulary."

Book Strand

Book strand 7, Objects and Places, includes this lesson in its diagram, pictured below. See page xiv for a complete description of this strand.

Objects and Places

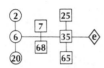

LESSON 66

The Wild, Wild West

Suggested Art Materials

See the art materials list for this lesson in the student book.

Planning Ahead

Ask the students to bring into class any visual examples they have which are representative of the Wild West era.

Helpful Teaching Hints

Discuss your students' examples and the pictures in the book in terms of the costumes, the modes of transportation, the buildings, and the landscapes depicted. Urge your students to always do extra research about any cultures whose styles they plan to employ in artworks. The result will be a better understanding of the reasons behind such styles and, thus, a better representation of the styles.

Book Strand

Book strand 11, Learning from Artists, includes this lesson in its diagram, pictured below. See page xv for a complete description of this strand.

Learning from Artists

LESSON 67

John Marin's New York

Suggested Art Materials

See the art materials list in the student book.

Planning Ahead

Collect photographs and paintings (abstract and realistic) of a variety of buildings.

Helpful Teaching Hints

- Use the pictures and photographs which you have collected to point out the three basic shapes which most buildings are composed of: the *cube*, the *cylinder*, and the *cone*. Discuss how both abstract and realistic renderings of buildings contain these shapes. Encourage the students to analyze buildings and natural objects in terms of these shapes as a preliminary to drawing.
- Review the principle of proportion so that the students' drawings will employ correct scale.

Book Strand

Book strand 1, Exploring with Paint, includes this lesson in its diagram, pictured below. See page xiii for a complete description of this strand.

Exploring with Paint

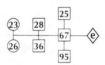

LESSON 68

I Know That Place

Suggested Art Materials

See the art materials list in the student book.

Helpful Teaching Hints

- Tell students that their sketchbooks should be useful to them for this lesson.
- Explain that a mixed media artwork often is effective for portraying a building, since different materials are used to build a single building.

Book Strand

Book strand 7, Objects and Places, includes this lesson in its diagram, pictured below. See page xiv for a complete description of this strand.

44

Objects and Places

```
        25
   2     |
   7 ─── 35 ──◇e
   6
  68     65
  20
```

LESSON 69

A Greek Temple

Suggested Art Materials

See the art materials list for this lesson in the student book.

Planning Ahead

For lessons 69–72, it is important for you to collect as many visuals as possible of the specific art styles to be discussed. You may want to make a display featuring plentiful examples of each style for students to look at throughout the remainder of the time spent on this unit.

Additional Materials Needed:

Materials for a bulletin board or display table; visuals of Greek, Roman, Middle Ages, Spanish, and Mexican architecture

Helpful Teaching Hints

- Compare Greek architecture with modern buildings, pointing out the ancient details that are still used today.
- Have the students spend plenty of time on their sketches before they attempt their final paintings.

Book Strand

Book strand 8, Buildings and Bridges, includes this lesson in its diagram, pictured at the top of the next column. See page xiv for a complete description of this strand.

Buildings and Bridges

```
        74
  69  71  |
   ┤   ├─ 76 ──◇e
  70  72
        78
```

LESSON 70

Roman Arches, Vaults, and Domes

Suggested Art Materials

See the art materials list for this lesson in the student book.

Helpful Teaching Hints

- Encourage the students to discuss their sketches with one another before they proceed to the finishing stages. They should be prepared to talk about the details of their buildings in terms of their purposes, and to justify the buildings' surroundings.
- Vanguard sheets or thin cardboard will work best for these models, as their strength and flexibility make constructing arches and domes easier.*

Additional Materials Needed:

* vanguard sheets or thin cardboard

Book Strand

Book strand 8, Buildings and Bridges, includes this lesson in its diagram, pictured below. See page xiv for a complete description of this strand.

Buildings and Bridges

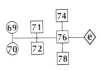

LESSON 71

Buildings in the Middle Ages

Suggested Art Materials

See the art materials list for this lesson in the student book.

Helpful Teaching Hints

This is an appropriate time to lead your class in a comparative study of various architectural forms. The display suggested in the guide to Lesson 69 will help you, but the thrust of the discussion should be the purposes behind the various architectural styles. Ask the students how the pictured structures did or did not meet their intended purposes.

Book Strand

Book strand 8, Buildings and Bridges, includes this lesson in its diagram, pictured below. See page xiv for a complete description of this strand.

Buildings and Bridges

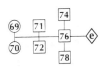

LESSON 72

Spanish Influences on Mexican Architecture

Suggested Art Materials

See the art materials list in the student book.

Helpful Teaching Hints

- After gaining experience by doing the last three lessons, the students should have little trouble drawing a building in a different setting for this lesson.
- Clay or plasticine is a useful medium for building models of structures like the Mayan Indians' temple pyramids. Time permitting, the students may wish to construct such models of their chosen buildings.*

Additional Materials Needed:
* clay or plasticine

Book Strand

Book strand 8, Buildings and Bridges, includes this lesson in its diagram, pictured below. See page xiv for a complete description of this strand.

Buildings and Bridges

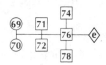

LESSON 73

Skeleton Architecture

Suggested Art Materials

See the art materials list in the student book.

Helpful Teaching Hints

- Refer the students to Lesson 60 (on armatures) as reinforcement for the contents of this lesson.
- Stress that the use of pencil alone should be sufficient for creating a finished drawing in this lesson.

Safety Precaution

Use glue only in a well-ventilated area.

Book Strand

Book strand 2, Creating with Lines, includes this lesson in its diagram, pictured below. See page xiii for a complete description of this strand.

Creating with Lines

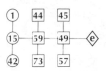

LESSON 74

Designing a Bridge

Suggested Art Materials

See the art materials list in the student book.

Helpful Teaching Hints

Requiring the students to place their bridges in environments lends a touch of authenticity to this lesson. Provide large sheets of plywood for the students to mount their models on and then decorate to resemble specific environments.
Additional Materials Needed:
large sheets of plywood

Safety Precaution

Use glue only in a well-ventilated area.

Book Strand

Book strand 8, Buildings and Bridges, includes this lesson in its diagram, pictured below. See page xiv for a complete description of this strand.

Buildings and Bridges

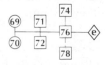

LESSON 75

Different Styles of American Architecture

Suggested Art Materials

See the art materials list in the student book.

Helpful Teaching Hints

- Allow the students to be as imaginative as they wish for this assignment, but also require them to be complete. Their drawings and models must include suitable details and surroundings.
- Encourage the students to be specific in their written descriptions of the buildings. Remind them that an understanding of the reasons behind details and features leads to greater appreciation of an architectural style.

Book Strand

Book strand 6, Near and Far, includes this lesson in its diagram, pictured below. See page xiv for a complete description of this strand.

Near and Far

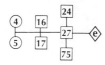

LESSON 76

Chicago Architecture

Suggested Art Materials

See the art materials list in the student book.

Helpful Teaching Hints

- Show visuals of the Chicago skyscape, and have each student choose a favorite building to research in terms of architect and influences. The student may choose to make a model of this building or another building by the same architect, or to simply create an original building.*
- Cardboard cartons in various sizes and shapes lend themselves quite easily to models of sky-scrapers.**

Additional Materials Needed:
  * visuals of the Chicago skyline
** cardboard cartons

Safety Precaution

Use glue only in a well-ventilated area.

Book Strand

Book strand 8, Buildings and Bridges, includes this lesson in its diagram, pictured below. See page xiv for a complete description of this strand.

Buildings and Bridges

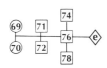

LESSON 77

The Architecture of Frank Lloyd Wright

Suggested Art Materials

See the art materials list in the student book.

Helpful Teaching Hints

- Compare the harmonious relationship between building and environment achieved by Frank Lloyd Wright to the more contrived and stylized architectural forms of some buildings. Discuss with the students what necessitates the latter style.
- If the students create models for this lesson, have them use natural found objects (stones, sticks, etc.).

Book Strand

Book strand 11, Learning from Artists, includes this lesson in its diagram, pictured below. See page xv for a complete description of this strand.

Learning from Artists

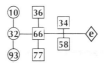

LESSON 78

Modern Architecture

Suggested Art Materials

See the art materials list in the student book.

Helpful Teaching Hints

At this point, it would be an exciting prospect to do a classroom project. Your class could create an entire model city which should include models of every type of building studied. The whole class should work together to plan the city, always relating the form of a building to its function. Then each student could create a model to contribute, and the whole class could work together to decorate the city.

Related Art Career (architect)

A career in architecture requires the most extensive education of all the art-related careers. A sound liberal arts base, including art, technical, and business courses followed by post-graduate work at an architecture school is necessary preparation for obtaining the required license to practice in most states. An architect both designs and supervises construction of buildings. The first step in designing a building is understanding its purpose and the needs of the people who will be using it. The architect must also know zoning laws and all other building codes and regulations for the area. A knowledge of construction materials and methods is also vital in preparing both the interior and exterior design of a building. In addition to the functional aspects of the building, an architect will combine aesthetic features into the design. Frank Lloyd Wright, a world-renowned architect, was able to maintain a high level of artistic creativity in the face of strong criticism towards his ideas, while at the same time fulfilling all of the technical requirements of his career.

As a class project, have students choose a single older building to redesign. They should also include street, walkway, lighting, and landscape features in their design. This may be done in a two-dimensional blue-print format or as a three-dimensional scale model.

Book Strand

Book strand 8, Buildings and Bridges, includes this lesson in its diagram, pictured below. See page xiv for a complete description of this strand.

Buildings and Bridges

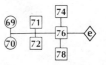

Exploring Art

Architecture in Action

See page 42 for an explanation and teaching suggestions.

Teacher's Notes

Unit VI
Explorations in Self-Expression

Learning Objectives

In this unit the students will achieve the following objectives:

Understanding Art

- Relate different art styles to the meanings behind them
- Understand the effects different media create
- Understand the power of imagination in art

Creating Art

- Study the artwork of famous artists and different cultures
- Make independent artistic choices
- Develop an individual art style and create artworks that express ideas and feelings

Appreciating Art

- Appreciate different styles of art as individual forms of expression
- Appreciate art as an emotional and creative outlet

Unit Strands

A strand consists of a group of related lessons where the student is expected to begin with one of the lesson choices available on the far left (arranged vertically), complete it, proceed horizontally to the next group of choices, make a choice and complete the lesson, and so forth, until the entire sequence has been completed. (See page v for complete instructions on using strands.) The unit strands for this unit are diagramed below.

Strand L: Messages and Imagination

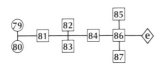

Strand M: Visual Discoveries

Background Information

Students like to be individualistic if given the encouragement. The lessons in Unit VI provide this opportunity. Although students are always urged to be imaginative and expressive in their work, you will find that the main thrust of these lessons is self-expression—as revealed both in the works of the masters and in the works of the students.

Through studying examples of works by many artists, the students learn about various forms of expression, from realistic to abstract. The students come to appreciate each art style as representing a unique point of view or feeling. This validates for the students their own emerging styles, and makes them feel more comfortable with using art to express feelings and emotions.

The classroom experience with different art techniques and media is also enlarged as the students complete the lessons in this unit. They are encouraged to experiment a great deal by using different media and modes of art expression. They are exposed to a variety of subject matter and asked to create works based on quite varied ideas. All of this experimentation and exposure leads to an expansion of the students' understanding of and experience with art.

Finally, this unit stresses the use of imagination. The non-realistic approaches of some of the lessons in the unit—the lessons on dream images, ghosts, creatures that never were, and robots—all help to develop the students' imaginations, while also validating the use of the fanciful in art.

What you, the teacher, can best add to these lessons is an atmosphere of acceptance and rapport that will enable the students to comfortably expose their feelings and creativity to you and to one another. With such an atmosphere, this unit can be an especially rewarding experience for your students.

Strategies for Motivation

Getting students to share their personal ideas and creativity becomes harder as the students grow older and more responsive to peer criticism. One way to encourage students to open up is to show them that an artist's personal side is often incorporated into his or her work. Sharing imagination thus becomes the norm rather than the exception.

Showing many imaginative examples also provides the students with ideas. It opens up the artistic realm to include all things, depicted in many ways. Students feel freer to experiment when they realize that new art styles are born out of experimentation.

The following areas are those to which the students probably need most exposure:
- abstract and Expressionistic art
- artworks based on dream imagery
- nonobjective art
- artists' statements about where they get their ideas for various works

Extending Art

Exploring Art

The Exploring Art feature for Unit VI encourages students to combine art skills with creative writing by composing and then illustrating a haiku poem. Begin by showing reproductions or slides of Japanese watercolor prints as you read haiku aloud to students. Discuss the economy of form and line that characterizes both the prints and the haiku. Then allow quiet time, preferably outdoors, for students to compose their haiku. Where sending students outdoors is impractical, nature photos from magazines (*Arizona Highways, National Geographic*) or books can also provide inspiration. Suggest that students try creating Japanese-style watercolors to illustrate their haiku. To further extend this lesson:
- Allow students to choose the media and styles they find most appropriate and to create series of illustrations for their favorite books. Students interested in creative writing may choose instead to illustrate stories or longer poems of their own.
- Assign students to write poems or short stories based on a work by a master artist, sculptor, or architect.

Additional Activities

Learning from first-hand experience is invaluable reinforcement for newly acquired knowledge. Once students understand and appreciate various styles of art, it is helpful for them to see real examples of the styles. Trips to museums and art galleries can provide this experience. However, if such field trips are impossible, the following suggestions will still broaden the students' interest and knowledge.

- Have the students organize an exhibit of their own work, dividing the "gallery" into categories and deciding which style each work represents.
- Have the students do in-depth reports (singly or in groups) on various art styles and the artists and works represented by the styles.
- Hold a class debate on the merits of objective versus nonobjective art.

Evaluating Procedures

As noted in the introduction to this book, evaluation in art classes poses unique problems for the teacher. (See pages vii-viii.) The *Learning Outcomes* address the need for self-evaluation and test the students on the details of what they have learned. However, the teacher still needs some means of determining the extent of a student's application of specifics to a solid core of basic art knowledge. Three things are involved in this type of evaluation:
1. A written test of the student's recall of important facts
2. An examination of the student's artwork in terms of the achievement of certain previously stated goals
3. An oral discussion with the student involving his or her comments on a particular piece of art.

These three evaluative components for Unit VI are explained below.

Vocabulary

Students who complete this unit should be able to define and correctly use the art terms listed below. A written test on the unit should, then, be based on these terms.

abstract	bestiary
anatomy	body proportions
assemblage	caricature
balance	creativity
distorted	pre-Columbian
express	Renaissance
Expressionism	rhythmic
haiku	symbolism
imagery	three-dimensional
image	title
medium	torso
negative	unity
positive	visualize

Skills

The artworks students create in this unit should meet the standards listed below. Be certain that the students are aware of these standards both as they plan and as they work. You may choose to keep this list posted throughout the time spent on this unit.

- The artwork conveys a definite meaning or feeling.
- The student's personal style is apparent, even though a particular artist's influence may be felt.
- Imagination is shown in the choice of media and subject matter.

Application of Knowledge

Listening to a student talk about an artwork can give you a true sense of how much the student understands the basic elements and principles of design. However, the planning behind such a discussion is important. First, the work to be discussed must be chosen in advance by the teacher. Questions must be written that will lead the student into the correct areas of emphasis. Last, the discussion should be arranged to take place on a one-to-one basis so that the more reticent students are not left out of a group discussion.

A suggested artwork to use for discussion purposes in this unit is the fanciful painting *Holiday on Wheels* by Graciela Rodo Boulanger.

Supplementary Materials and Resources

Chapman, Dr. Laura. *Discover Art*. Worcester, MA: David Publications, Inc., 1984.
This book helps to teach students how to look at art, live with art, and create art.

Roukes, Nicholas. *Art Synetics*. Worcester, MA: Davis Publications, Inc., 1984.
This book, in six interesting chapters, encourages the type of creative thinking which transforms everyday objects into new and unusual structures.

TEACHING SUGGESTIONS for Lessons 79–95

LESSON 79

Peace and Tranquillity

Suggested Art Materials

See the art materials list for this lesson in the student book.

Helpful Teaching Hints

- Have the students jot down the things that come to mind when they think of peace. Remind them that peace can be portrayed in the subject matter as well as in the techniques and media used.

- When discussing artworks that portray peace, it is best to begin with pictorial images and then to move on to abstract images. Discuss these artworks in terms of color, use of line and shape, and subject matter.

Book Strand

Book strand 9, Artistic Messages, includes this lesson in its diagram, pictured below. See page xiv for a complete description of this strand.

Artistic Messages

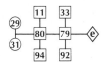

LESSON 80

Dream Images

Suggested Art Materials

See the art materials list for this lesson in the student book.

Planning Ahead

Show reproductions of paintings by Dali, Miro, and Max Ernst. Discuss the dreamlike qualities of these works.

Helpful Teaching Hints

- Point out in the examples in the text and in the reproductions used above some of the ways that a dreamlike quality is achieved: fantasy, distortion, exaggeration, strange color schemes.
- Have the students write brief summaries of their dreams and display them next to the pictures.

Safety Precaution

Use glue only in a well-ventilated area.

Book Strands

Book strand 9, Artistic Messages, and book strand 13, Fantasy and Distortion, include this lesson in their diagrams, pictured below. See pages xiv and xv, respectively, for complete descriptions of these strands.

Artictic Messages   Fantasy and Distortion

   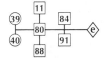

LESSON 81

An Expression of You

Suggested Art Materials

See the art materials list in the student book.

Planning Ahead

Have the students bring in pictures of themselves. These can be displayed next to the paintings they create for this lesson.

Helpful Teaching Hints

- Have examples of portraiture from the Expressionistic era available for students to study. These examples will give them some ideas on how to approach their own attempts at Expressionistic self-portraits.*
- Students may enjoy using distorted grids to create Expressionistic self-portraits:
(1) Cut up the picture of yourself.
(2) Space the pieces out in odd ways.
(3) Draw in the lines connecting the various pieces.
(4) Transfer the results to a clean page, using the grid system.
(5) Paint the picture in the Expressionistic style.
Additional Materials Needed:
* portraiture from the Expressionistic era

Book Strand

Book strand 10, Visions and Feelings, includes this lesson in its diagram, pictured at the top of the next column. See page xv for a complete description of this strand.

Visions and Feelings

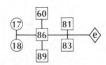

LESSON 82

From Real to Abstract

Suggested Art Materials

See the art materials list for this lesson in the student book.

Helpful Teaching Hints

- Students can use the grid system (explained in the

previous lesson) to achieve abstract results for this lesson.
- Students can create Cubist pictures by drawing and painting different views of the same object within a single composition—either juxtaposing the views or connecting them.

Safety Precaution

Use glue only in a well-ventilated area.

Book Strands

Book strand 5, Contrast and Opposites, and book strand 14, The Road to Abstraction, include this lesson in their diagrams, pictured below. See pages xiv and xv, respectively, for complete descriptions of these strands.

Contrast and Opposites   The Road to Abstraction

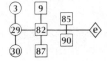   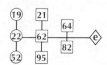

LESSON 83

Be Your Own Picasso

Suggested Art Materials

See the art materials list in the student book.

Planning Ahead

You will want to preface this lesson with a brief lecture on Picasso's life. Point out the relationship between the events in his life and the development of his style. You may wish to discuss his periods and show examples of each.
Additional Materials Needed:
resources (visual and written) featuring Picasso

Helpful Teaching Hints

- Encourage the students to respond honestly to Picasso's work. Ask them to explain their likes or dislikes.
- You might wish to instruct the students to use ideas from Picasso's paintings in their own efforts. Their final products will reveal their interpretations and impressions of his work.

Book Strand

Book strand 10, Visions and Feelings, includes this lesson in its diagram, pictured below. See page xv for a complete description of this strand.

Visions and Feelings

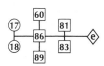

LESSON 84

Impossible Imaginings

Suggested Art Materials

See the art materials list in the student book.

Helpful Teaching Hints

Make sure the students understand that the artists discussed in this lesson are accepted as masters. Verify that fanciful subject matter is not taken lightly; such images can often be powerful and dynamic.

Book Strand

Book strand 13, Fantasy and Distortion, includes this lesson in its diagram, pictured below. See page xv for a complete description of this strand.

Fantasy and Distortion

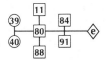

LESSON 85

Unexpected Ghosts

Suggested Art Materials

See the art materials list for this lesson in the student book.

Helpful Teaching Hints

Negatives can be projected on a wall or screen to dramatize the concept of this lesson.
Additional Materials Needed:
overhead projector, negatives

Related Art Careers (photographer and filmmaker)

The works of photographer Ansel Adams displayed in art galleries and assembled in books confirm photography as a major artform. Photography is now taught in many design colleges, and includes a combination of basic art courses, liberal arts, and training in the technology of the camera.

Have students look through a variety of magazines, noting the different uses for photography (e.g., advertisements and story illustrations). Discuss the differences between photography and other comparable commercial art careers (graphic design, book illustration, etc.).

A new, related field is that of filmmaking. It is costly, highly technical, and heavily unionized. Education might include courses in video, cinematography, graphic design, and photography. Fine arts, make-up, and history of costuming and drama are also helpful. There is great demand for filmmakers outside the major film industry in such fields as education, industry, commercials, and computer-generated graphics.

Have students watch an educational or commercial video and note the various job titles listed in the credits. Ask students to select a job title that interests them and research it for required education and skills. Have the students share this information with the entire class.

Book Strand

Book strand 5, Contrast and Opposites, includes this lesson in its diagram, pictured below. See page xiv for a complete description of this strand.

Contrast and Opposites

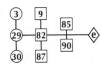

LESSON 86

The Land of Lilliput

Suggested Art Materials

See the art materials list in the student book.

Planning Ahead

Begin the class by having the students study cross sections of vegetables for five minutes. Ask them to note down all the details they see. See who makes the longest list.
Additional Materials Needed:
pieces of raw vegetables

Helpful Teaching Hints

An interesting twist to this lesson is to have all the students draw their designs after studying the same picture. See how different the results are, and discuss how this shows variety in imagination and artistic vision.

Additional Materials Needed:
slide or transparency of magnified natural object, slide projector or overhead projector

Book Strand

Book strand 10, Visions and Feelings, includes this lesson in its diagram, pictured below. See page xv for a complete description of this strand.

Visions and Feelings

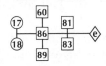

LESSON 87

Night and Day

Suggested Art Materials

See the art materials list for this lesson in the student book.

Helpful Teaching Hints

- Studying photographs of the same scene taken during day and night can help students see exactly what kinds of changes take place.*
- An alternative way for students to experiment with the effects of different lighting is to have them draw a series of still lifes. For the first attempt, have them draw the still life as it appears in the regular classroom lighting. For the second attempt, turn off the lights and cast flood lamps on the still life. For the third attempt, use blue lighting or even black lights for different effects. (Be sure to set up the still life using objects with definite planes and different sizes and shapes. This will cause the light to play a more dramatic role.)**

Additional Materials Needed:
  * photographs of night and day scenes
  ** still life objects, flood lamps, blue lights, black lights

Book Strand

Book strand 5, Contrast and Opposites, includes this lesson in its diagram, pictured below. See page xiv for a complete description of this strand.

Contrast and Opposites

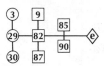

LESSON 88

Art in Motion

Suggested Art Materials

See the art materials list for this lesson in the student book.

Helpful Teaching Hints

Here is a simple way to show motion in art:
(1) Draw the object or person that you want to portray as moving.
(2) Cut the drawing out along its outer edges.
(3) Trace around the edges of the cutout. Now gradually shift the cutout so it is slightly off the original registration. Trace it again.
(4) Repeat as many times as you wish.
Once the students see how this illusion of movement works, they should attempt to show motion freehand.

Book Strand

Book strand 13, Fantasy and Distortion, includes this lesson in its diagram, pictured below. See page xv for a complete description of this strand.

Fantasy and Distortion

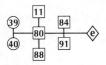

LESSON 89

Robots in Art

Suggested Art Materials

See the art materials list for this lesson in the student book.

Planning Ahead

Begin this lesson by inviting the class to discuss their

favorite video games. Have them describe the characters, special effects, and futuristic objects featured in these games.

Helpful Teaching Hints

- Discuss the robots featured in the student text. How would the students change the robots? What reasons do they give for these changes?
- Asking the students to give their robots names and assigned functions will cause the students to plan their designs more carefully.

Safety Precautions

Use spray paints and glue only in a well-ventilated area.

Related Art Career (industrial designer)

Industrial designers are creative problem solvers. They combine technical knowledge of methods, materials, and machines with design talent to create or improve the appearance or function of machine-made products. Part designers, technicians, and merchandisers, they work between industry and the consumer to improve our standard of living. A college education combining courses in graphic design, photography, architecture, illustration, engineering, and crafts will prepare the industrial designer for this diverse career. The starting position is usually model-maker or draftsperson, often called a technical illustrator.

Ask students to bring in products that have been designed by industrial designers, such as a metal and plastic clothes hanger, brown paper bag and new plastic grocery bag, toothpaste tube and new dispenser, aluminum and glass soft drink containers, a cake of hand soap and liquid dispensed soap. Compare and discuss changes and improvements and overall effectiveness of the product designs. Did the new products improve our standard of living? Then have students invent their own industrial designs.

Book Strand

Book strand 10, Visions and Feelings, includes this lesson in its diagram, pictured below. See page xv for a complete description of this strand.

Visions and Feelings

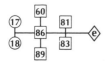

LESSON 90

Pets and Their People

Suggested Art Materials

See the art materials list in the student book.

Helpful Teaching Hints

- Stress that, for this lesson, students should use realistic subject matter. This could, in fact, turn into a lesson on close observation.
- If the students are drawing their own pets, ask them to make sketches first and to spend time observing. If the students are depicting unusual pets, ask them to collect and study pictures of the animals (encyclopedias are good sources). Encourage the students to include details characteristic of each animal's nature and of the mood of the artwork.

Book Strand

Book strand 5, Contrast and Opposites, includes this lesson in its diagram, pictured below. See page xiv for a complete description of this strand.

Contrast and Opposites

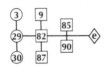

LESSON 91

Creatures That Never Were

Suggested Art Materials

See the art materials list for this lesson in the student book.

Planning Ahead

Comic strips based on science fiction and the covers of science fiction books often show good examples of fantastic creatures. Ask your students to bring to class any such examples which they have.

Helpful Teaching Hints

Students might enjoy making "collage animals." They could use parts of magazine photos, bits of material or foil, natural objects, and their own added details to create really fantastic creatures.

Additional Materials Needed:

magazines, collage materials

Book Strand

Book strand 13, Fantasy and Distortion, includes this lesson in its diagram, pictured below. See page xv for a complete description of this strand.

Fantasy and Distortion

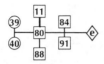

LESSON 92

Images of Heroes

Suggested Art Materials

See the art materials list for this lesson in the student book.

Helpful Teaching Hints

• Discuss with the students what characteristics they think a hero should have. Such oral identification of characteristics and qualities will make it easier for the students to transfer their feelings into art.

• Ask the students to carefully consider what kinds of activities their heroes are or should be involved in. This will help them choose appropriate ways of depicting the heroes.

Book Strand

Book strand 9, Artistic Messages, includes this lesson in its diagram, pictured below. See page xiv for a complete description of this strand.

Artistic Messages

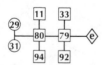

LESSON 93

Larger than Life

Suggested Art Materials

See the art materials list for this lesson in the student book.

Planning Ahead

Bring in a copy of *Gray's Anatomy* (available at most

libraries) for students to thumb through. Once they realize how extensive the field of anatomy is, they will better understand the breadth of Michelangelo's genius.
Additional Materials Needed:
Gray's Anatomy

Helpful Teaching Hints

Encourage your students by telling them that correct depiction of bodily proportions is one of the hardest skills to achieve in art. Praise them for showing an understanding of proportion and for trying to use it.

Book Strand

Book strand 11, Learning from Artists, includes this lesson in its diagram, pictured below. See page xv for a complete description of this strand.

Learning from Artists

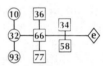

LESSON 94

Visualizing with Words

Suggested Art Materials

See the art materials list in the student book.

Helpful Teaching Hints

Simplify this lesson by having the students think of an important experience and the one word they would use to describe the experience or the feelings the experience caused them to have. The related artwork could then be based on this single word.

Book Strand

Book strand 9, Artistic Messages, includes this lesson in its diagram, pictured below. See page xiv for a complete description of this strand.

Artistic Messages

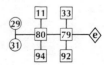

LESSON 95

Songs, Poetry, and Art

Suggested Art Materials

See the art materials list for this lesson in the student book.

Planning Ahead

Select some of your favorite poetry and prose to read aloud to your students.
Additional Materials Needed:
literary excerpts

Helpful Teaching Hints

• Begin the lesson by reading aloud to your students. Ask them to doodle or sketch whatever comes to mind as you are reading. Their pencils should not stop moving while you are reading. (This exercise should loosen their creativity and put their minds in a relaxed state receptive to imaginative ideas.)

• Point out to the students that imagery and symbolism are equally important to writers and artists.

Book Strands

Book strand 1, Exploring with Paint, and book strand 14, The Road to Abstraction, include this lesson in their diagrams, pictured below. See pages xiii and xv, respectively, for complete descriptions of these strands.

Exploring with Paint

The Road to Abstraction

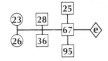

Exploring Art

Writing and Illustrating Haiku

See page 50 for an explanation and teaching suggestions.

Teacher's Notes

SUPPLIES CHART*

Supplies/Lesson Number	1	2	3	4	5	6	7	8	9	10	11	12	13	14	15	16	17	18	19	20	21	22	23	24	25	26
Brayer										F				F					F	F						
Brushes										R				R					R	R	•	•	•	•	•	•
Calligraphy tools										E				E					E	E						
Cardboard										E				E					E	E						
Chalk																									•	
Clay										C				C					C	C						
Construction paper										H				H					H	H					•	
Cutting tools										O				O					O	O						
Dowel										I				I					I	I						
Drawing instruments										C				C	•				C	C						
Fabric										E				E					E	E						
Foil																										
Glue																•									•	
Hammer and nails																										
Ink																									•	
Knife																										
Linoleum																										
Magazines							•				•					•										
Magnifying glass					•							•														
Markers	•			•																					•	
Mixing tray																					•	•	•	•	•	•
Modeling tools																										
Natural objects						•																				
Plastic bags																										
Pliers																										
Pens	•			•							•															
Printer's ink																										
Rasp																										
Rolling pin																										
Ruler														•	•	•										
Sandpaper																										
Scissors																•										
Slip																										
String		•																								
Tacks														•												
Tape	•						•					•				•										•
Tapestry needle																										
Tempera paint																					•	•	•	•	•	
Thread																										
Toothpicks																										
Watercolor paints																									•	
Wheat paste																										
Wire																										
Wire cutters																										
Wood (boards)																									•	
Yarn		•																								

*The following items are needed in nearly every lesson, and so are not included on the chart: pencil and eraser, white drawing or sketching paper, newspaper, water, and paper towels.

Supplies/Lesson Number	27	28	29	30	31	32	33	34	35	36	37	38	39	40	41	42	43	44	45	46	47	48	49	50	51
Brayer																					●				
Brushes	●	●	●	●	●	●	●	●	●	●											●	●		●	●
Calligraphy tools																							●		
Cardboard																									
Chalk													●				●								
Clay																				●					
Construction paper											●	●					●				●			●	
Cutting tools																									
Dowel																	●		●						
Drawing instruments																									
Fabric												●			●	●	●								
Foil																									●
Glue											●	●		●										●	●
Hammer and nails																				●					●
Ink					●							●										●	●		●
Knife																									
Linoleum																					●				
Magazines													●	●						●					
Magnifying glass																									
Markers												●										●		●	
Mixing tray	●	●	●	●	●	●	●	●	●	●	●											●		●	
Modeling tools																									●
Natural objects																		●		●					
Plastic bags	●																								
Pliers																									
Pens																									
Printer's ink																					●				
Rasp																									
Rolling pin																									
Ruler													●		●								●	●	
Sandpaper																									
Scissors											●		●	●	●	●	●	●	●	●				●	
Slip																									
String																		●		●					●
Tacks																									
Tape	●																								
Tapestry needle															●	●	●								
Tempera paint		●	●	●			●	●	●	●											●	●		●	
Thread																	●			●					
Toothpicks																									
Watercolor paints	●	●	●	●	●	●	●	●	●	●												●		●	
Wheat paste																				●					
Wire																				●					
Wire cutters																									
Wood (boards)																									●
Yarn															●	●		●	●						

Supplies/Lesson Number	52	53	54	55	56	57	58	59	60	61	62	63	64	65	66	67–72	73	74	75	76	77	78	79	80	81
Brayer														F		F			F		F			F	
Brushes	•										•			R	•	R			R	•	R	•	•	R	•
Calligraphy tools														E		E			E		E			E	
Cardboard	•									•				E		E		•	E	•	E			E	
Chalk																									
Clay			•	•	•				•	•	•	•	•	C		C	•	•	C		C			C	
Construction paper														H		H			H		H			H	
Cutting tools														O		O			O		O			O	
Dowel														I		I			I		I			I	
Drawing instruments														C		C			C		C			C	
Fabric														E		E			E		E			E	
Foil																									
Glue	•	•				•											•	•		•					
Hammer and nails																									
Ink																									
Knife			•		•					•	•	•	•												
Linoleum																									
Magazines															•			•			•				
Magnifying glass																									
Markers																				•	•				
Mixing tray	•										•									•		•	•		•
Modeling tools				•					•	•															
Natural objects													•												
Plastic bags			•	•	•					•							•								
Pliers							•	•																	
Pens																				•		•			
Printer's ink																									
Rasp											•	•	•												
Rolling pin				•																					
Ruler																									
Sandpaper						•					•	•	•												
Scissors	•				•	•	•										•	•							
Slip				•																					
String						•	•		•									•							
Tacks						•																			
Tape		•					•		•																
Tapestry needle																									
Tempera paint	•														•					•		•	•		•
Thread																									
Toothpicks																	•	•		•					
Watercolor paints													•							•		•	•		•
Wheat paste								•																	
Wire						•	•	•	•									•							
Wire cutters						•	•	•	•																
Wood (boards)						•			•																
Yarn						•																			

Supplies/Lesson Number	82	83	84	85	86	87	88	89	90–94	95
Brayer		F	F		F		F		F	
Brushes		R	R	•	R	•	R	•	R	•
Calligraphy tools		E	E		E		E		E	
Cardboard		E	E		E		E		E	
Chalk										
Clay		C	C		C	•	C		C	
Construction paper	•	H	H		H		H		H	
Cutting tools		O	O		O		O		O	
Dowel		I	I		I		I		I	
Drawing instruments		C	C		C		C		C	
Fabric		E	E		E		E		E	
Foil								•		
Glue	•							•		•
Hammer and nails										
Ink										
Knife						•				
Linoleum										
Magazines	•			•						
Magnifying glass										
Markers				•						
Mixing tray				•		•		•		•
Modeling tools										
Natural objects										
Plastic bags										
Pliers										
Pens				•						
Printer's ink										
Rasp										
Rolling pin										
Ruler										
Sandpaper										
Scissors										
Slip										
String										
Tacks										
Tape								•		
Tapestry needle	•									
Tempera paint				•		•		•		•
Thread										
Toothpicks								•		
Watercolor paints				•		•		•		•
Wheat paste										
Wire										
Wire cutters										
Wood (boards)										
Yarn										

Teacher's Notes